Holy Days: The Historic and Paga Holiday Celebrations

By Timothy Medsker

Holy Days: The Historic and Pagan Origins of Modern Day Holiday Celebrations

All Scripture taken from the VW Edition (www.a-voice.org)

ISBN 978-0-9906958-3-7

Holy Days: The Historic and Pagan Origins of Modern Day Holiday Celebrations

Contents

Introduction

Holiday (Holy Day)

Originally, a religious anniversary; now, a day set apart for exemption from labor or for a formal or informal celebration.

Webster's University Dictionary Unabridged, 1942

American society is engrained with the celebration of holidays, as well as every other country in the world. The difference with celebrations in the United States are that they tend to nowadays be much more commercialized and less religious than celebrations that take place in different cultures around the world. It was America that popularized Santa Claus into the widely recognized images of the man in the red suit, much due to Coca Cola's advertising.

Nearly every holiday or holy day has an origin that is far from what is publicly perceived. In nearly every non-national holiday there are pagan origins that explain much of the common day celebrations that take place with these holy days. There are reasons that there is an Easter bunny, a Christmas tree and even Christmas lights. Some of these pagan origins were supposedly Christianized, however, it is not possible to take something that is inherently evil and make it good.

My family and I celebrated each and every holiday, just as most Americans do currently. For years I was heavily engrained in all of the popular customs associated with these holidays, at both home and church. One day I met a man who told me about the origins of Christmas, how it was a pagan celebration. As a Christian I had to see if these things were so.

I had been of the "put Christ back in Christmas" crowd. Already I was beginning to frown heavily upon Santa Claus and all of the mass marketing that took place each and every holiday season. I wasn't against Christmas gifts, but was against the lack of focus on

4

Christ. How many of those who celebrated this holiday even thought of Jesus once throughout the day? However, when this man who claimed to be a Christian told me of these things, I knew that the only way I could put my mind to rest about these claims was to do the research myself.

In the year 2000 I headed off to many libraries around the Chicago area, scouring books to see what the origins of Christmas might be. I began to find a trend. Most of the books that were written from around 1950 and up, agreed with what I had learned growing up regarding customs of Christmas. On the other hand, most all of the books prior to 1950 told of a darker origin of Christmas. It was then that I decided in order to get to the root of the matter I would find the oldest books on the subject that I could find.

I managed to find several books, some printed in the late 1800's, that told a story of pagan origins and attributed those origins to many of the popular customs held regarding the celebration of Christmas. At that moment I knew my friend was correct in what he told me, indeed there were pagan origins of Christmas. I took my research further, now with a curiosity of wondering what other things I celebrated or other customs I participated in were also of pagan origins.

This led to further eye opening research that showed a lot of superstitious and pagan practices are hidden by a thin veil in our modern culture. As a Christian I chose to sustain from doing these things. In this book, which is a collection of articles that I had originally typed up, I will present to you, the reader, my findings from the research I have done. The focus will be on holidays that have mostly religious origins. Halloween and May Day are excluded from this book, the origins of those holy days should be quite obvious to a true follower of Christ.

Tim Medsker

Chapter 1

New Year's Day

We are going to take a relatively comprehensive look at the origins of New Year's Day. This historical study will also include some information on New Year's Eve as these two go hand and hand. We will specifically look at the historical origins of past years and compare those with the current traditions that are now celebrated.

For this historical portion of the study we will not be using any internet resources. The only resources that will be used are from old books. So let's begin…

January's "beginning being near the winter solstice, the year is thus made to present a complete series of the seasonal changes and operations, including equally the first movements of spring, and the death of the annual vegetation in the frozen arms of winter. Yet the earliest calendars, as the Jewish, the Egyptian, and Greek, did not place the commencement of the year at this point. It was not done till the formation of the Roman calendar, usually attributed to the second king, Numa Pompilus, whose reign is set down as terminating anno 672 B.C. Numa, it is said, having decreed that the year should commence now, added two new months to the ten into which the year had previously been divided, calling the first Januarius, in honour of Janus, the deity supposed to preside over doors (Lat. Janua, a door), who might very naturally be resumed also to have something to do with the opening of the year."[1] "The ancient Jewish year, which opened with the 25th of March, continued long to have a legal position in Christian countries. In England, it was not till 1752 that the 1st of January became the initial day of the legal."[2] "In Soctland, this desirable change was made by a decrees of James VI. In privy council, in the year 1600. It was effected in France in 1564; in Holland, Protestant Germany, and Russia, in 1700; and in Sweden in 1753."[3]

'Long ere the lingering dawn of that blithe morn
Which ushers in the year, the roosting cock,

Flapping his wings, repeats his larum shrill;
But on that morn no busy flail obeys
His rousing call; no sounds but sounds of joy
Salute the year – the first-foot's entering step,
That sudden on the floor is welcome heard,
Ere blushing maids have braided up their hair;
The laugh, the hearty kiss, the good new year
Pronounced with honest warmth. In village, grauge,
And borough town, the steaming flagon, borne
From house to house, elates the poor man's heart,
And makes him feel that life has still its joys.
The aged and the young, man, woman, child,
Unite in social glee; even stranger dogs,
Meeting with bristling back, soon lay aside
Their snarling aspect, and in sportive chase,
Excursive scour, or wallow in the snow.
With sober cheerfulness, the grandma eyes
Her offspring round her, all in health and peace;
And, thankful that she's spared to see this day
Return once more, breathes low a secret prayer,
That God would shed a blessing on their heads.'

Grahame.[4]

Staying up until midnight to cheer Happy New Year has been a custom for quite some time. New Year's resolutions have been made by many for some time also. "The merrymakings of New-Year's Eve and New-Year's Day are of very ancient date in England."[5] Toasting a drink on New Year's Eve is also an old custom. "A double-handled flagon full of sweetened and spiced wine being handed to the master, or other person presiding, he drinks standing to the general health, as announced by the toastmaster; then passes it to his neighbor on the left hand, who drinks standing to this next neighbor, also standing, as so on it goes, till all have drunk."[6] We are going to once again turn to explanations regarding why New Year's Day is on the 1st of January.

"The ancient Egyptians began their year on September 21, the date of the autumn equinox, and the ancient Greeks began their year on June 21, the date of the summer solstice. For a short time December 25 was the date of the beginning of the year in New England."[7] "After December 25 had been fixed as the day of the nativity, the church made January 1 a religious festival in commemoration of the circumcision of Jesus."[8] "It was on account of the orgies which accompanied the recurrence of the winter solstice not only among the Romans but among the Teutonic races that the early Christians looked with scant favor upon the whole season. By the fifth century, however, the 25 of December had become a fixed festival commemorative of our Lord's Nativity, whereupon the 1st of January assumed a specially sacred character as the octave of Christmas Day and the anniversary of Christ's circumcision."[14] It should well be noted that according to the Holy Scriptures males where circumcised eight days after they were born. Including the 25th of December it would be indeed eight days later New Year's Day. However, we know that Jesus was not born on the 25th of December. In fact this might explain why Christmas is celebrated on the 25th of December, rather than on the winter solstice's actual date of December 21st.

"So it was, on the eighth day, that they came to circumcise the child..." Luke 1:59a

George Washington, Thomas Jefferson and other Presidents used to open their houses to receive people. According to a Senator at the time, "made the President the compliments of the season; had a hearty shake of the hand. I was asked to partake of the punch and cakes, but declined. I sat down and we had some chat. But the diplomatic gentry and foreigners coming in, I embraced the first vacancy to make my bow and wish him a good morning."[9]

"Among the Romans, after the reformation of the calendar, the first day of January, as well as the entire month, was dedicated to the eponymic god Janus. He was represented with two faces, on looking forward, the other backward, to indicate that he stood between the old and the new year, with a regard to both. Throughout January the Romans offered sacrifices to Janus upon twelve altars."[11] "Ovid and other Latin writers of the Empire allude to the suspension of all litigation and strife, the reconciliation of differences between friends, the smoking altars and the white-robed processions to the Capitol, upon the first day of Janus, or New Year's Day as we now call it. They also tell of the exchanging of visits, the giving and receiving of presents, the masquerading and the feasting, with which in their time the day was celebrated throughout the Roman Empire."[12]

There was also a custom of handing out gifts on New Year's Day in parts of Europe. People used to give gifts to the royalty, there were also those who would go door to door (usually a group of boys) to get money or food. Gifts would also be handed out to certain guests at their home. "The stenae (gifts) were not only exchanged between relatives and friends, but were exacted by the Emperors from their subjects. Eventually they became so onerous a burden to the people that Claudius limited their cost by a decree."[13] However the Druids all had done this. "The Druids distributed branches of the sacred mistletoe, cut with peculiar ceremonies, as New Year's gifts to the people."[10] "The Persians celebrated the beginning of the year by exchanging presents of eggs."[16] However this custom of gift giving, at least nowadays, does not exist in America. "The custom of exchanging presents on New Year's, though in Anglo-Saxon countries it has been largely superseded by the giving of Christmas-gifts, is still retained in France and the Latin countries (as when this was written)."[15]

Christians should understand that all of our months and days of the week are named after Roman gods. After all it is the Roman calendar that most of the world uses today. So this study of New Year's Day has perhaps revealed the reason for December 25 being selected as the celebrated birthday of Jesus, if nothing else. Truly many in our society celebrate New Year's Eve with drunkenness and all other sorts of debauchery. Perhaps our generation is worse in many respects than those past societies of old?

Chapter 2

St. Patrick's Day

This time we are going to investigate the origins of St. Patrick's Day. During this investigation we will try and discover the origin for the mandate to wear green, the symbolic significance of the leprechaun and clover. For this historical study we are going to reference one old book regarding the historical significance of this that and see if we can get to the bottom of it. Let's begin...

A Historical Peek...

St. Patrick's Day is celebrated in March, but where did this holiday (holy day) start. St. Patrick "was born about the year 372, and when only sixteen years of age, was carried off by pirates, who sold him into slavery in Ireland; where his master employed him as a swineherd on the well-known mountain of Sleamish, in the county of Antrim. Here he passed seven years, during which time he acquired a knowledge of the Irish language, and made himself acquainted with the manners, habits, and customs of the people. Escaping from captivity, and, after many adventures, reaching the Continent, he was successively ordained deacon, priest, and bishop; and then once more, with the authority of Pope Celestine, he returned to Ireland to preach the Gospel to its then heathen inhabitants."[1] Here as with all previous historical study supplements we see once again Rome having played a hand in the origin of yet another celebrated American holiday.

St. Patrick has many supposed miracles attributed to him that appear to be originated the same as pagan legends. A few of those include, starting a fire using ice and gently blow on it, casting all of the snakes out of Ireland, and cursing the Druids. Many towns, ports and other points of interest in the area derive there name in one form or another including that of St. Patrick. St. Patrick started a couple of churches, including one in Dublin. Finally "he is commonly stated to have died at Saul on the 17th of March 493, in the one hundred and twenty-first year of his age."[2]

Now the clover, known as the shamrock, "the well-known trefoil plant, and Irish national emblem, is almost universally worn in the hat over all Ireland, on St. Patrick's Day. The popular notion is, that when St. Patrick was preaching the doctrine of the Trinity to the pagan Irish, he used this plane, bearing three leaves upon one stem, as a symbol or illustration of the great mystery."[3] "The trefoil in Arabic is called shamrakh, and was held sacred in Iran as emblematical of the Persian Triads."[4] Another point of interest regarding this holiday deals with Noah.

"The early English calendars pretend that on the 17th of March Noah entered the ark."[5] A very interesting piece of history that both the entering of the ark and St. Patrick's Day would have been observed on the same day. This sums up our brief look into St. Patrick's Day. While the origin of the leprechaun and wearing of green is unknown and may very well have been added in the not-so-distant past we can once again observe that this holiday is associated with a Roman Catholic saint. A true Christian's basic doctrine goes against that of the Roman Catholic church (RCC) and therefore holidays that glorify their saints should not be observed.

Chapter 3

Groundhog Day

Groundhog day is certainly not a holiday that many celebrate. Yet every year there is an event that takes place in Punxsutawney, PA. This has been going on since 1886. According to groundhog.org, the official website of the event, "if Punxsutawney Phil sees his shadow, there will be six more weeks of winter weather. If he does not see his shadow, there will be an early spring." This site admits that the origins of this event are from the Catholic Candlemas (at the time this was written). So just what are the origins of Candlemas? This study will take a brief look into the origins of Groundhog Day.

A Historical Look

"From a very early, indeed unknown date in the Christian history, the 2nd of February has been held as the festival of the Purification of the Virgin, and it is still a holiday of the Church of England."[1] The popular name of Candlemas is derived from the ceremony which the Church of Rome dictates to be observed on this day; namely, a blessing of candles by the clergy..."[2] "At Rome, the Pope every year officiates at this festival in the beautiful chapel of the Quirinal. When he has blessed the candles, he distributes them with his own hand amongst those in the church...The cardinals go first; then follow the bishops, canons, priors, abbots, priests, down to the sacristans and meanest officers of the church"[3]

"It appears that in England, in Catholic times, a meaning was attached to the size of the candles and the manner in which they burned during the procession; that, moreover, the reserved parts of the candles were deemed to posses a strong supernatural virtue:

'This done, each man his candle lights,
Where chiefest seemeth he,
Whose taper greatest may be seen;
And fortunate to be,

Whose candles burneth clear and bright:
A wondrous force and might
Doth in these candles lie, which if
At any time they light,
They sure believe that neither storm
Nor tempest doth abide,
Nor thunder in the skies be heard,
Nor any devil's spide,
Nor fearful sprites that walk by night,
Nor hurts of frost or hail'"[4]

There is more to be learned regarding this custom and it's relation to the Roman Catholic Church and the Purification of Mary. However the focus of this brief historical study is focusing on Candlemas's relationship to Groundhog Day, to where we will once again continue in that direction. "There is a universal superstition throughout Christendom, that good weather on this day indicates a long continuance of winter and a bad crop, and that its being foul is, on the contrary, a good omen. Sir Thomas Browne, in his Vulgar Errors, quotes a Latin distich expressive of this idea; which may be considered as well translated in the popular Scottish rhyme:

'If Candlemas day be dry and fair,
The half o' winter's to come and mair;
If Candlemas be wet and foul,
The half o'winter's gane at Yule."[5]

Germany had a couple of proverbial expressions about Candlemas day. One goes as follows, "The badger peeps out of his hole on Candlemas day, and when he finds snow, walks abroad; but if he sees the sun shining, he draws back into his hole."[6]

These notions, like Candlemas, "are derived from pagan times." In Martin's Description of the Western Islands, on Candlemas day "the Hebrideans observe the following curious custom: 'The mistress and servants of each family take a sheaf of oats and dress it up in women's apparel, put it in a large basket, and lay a wooden club by it, and this they call Brud's Bed; and then the mistress and servants cry three times, "Brud is come; Brud is welcome!" This they do just before going to bed, and when they rise in the morning they look among the ashes, expecting to see the impression of Brud's club there; which, if they do, they reckon it a true presage of a good crop and prosperous year, and the contrary they take as an ill omen."[7]

The customs of Groundhog Day was brought to America by Great Britain and Germany. "In Germany it was the badger which broke its hibernation to observe the skies, in the United States the belief was transferred to the woodchuck."[8] So there is a brief history of Groundhog Day. This American take on Groundhog Day apparently has origins that go back to at least Candlemas in Europe and further elsewhere.

Chapter 4

Good Friday

This is a particularly important study as we dive into the origins of celebrated holidays, regarding Easter, Palm Sunday and Good Friday. This study will take a comprehensive look at these holidays (holy days) utilizing mostly old books, one new book and two online resources. While all roads seem to lead to Rome regarding the origins of holidays, this one is the most important one to understand the origins. While Christians are to remember Resurrection Sunday as the day that our Lord and Savior Jesus Christ rose from the dead, we must be certain that our practices during this time of the year do not blaspheme the Most High and His Son. So lets begin...

We are going to start with Good Friday and some common sense. Jesus rose from the dead on a Sunday, three days after His death. So going backwards we would go Saturday, Friday, Thursday. If you went to a job interview on a Monday and they told you to come back in three days, which day would you show up? Thursday of course. So why Good Friday?

"For I delivered to you first of all that which I also received: that Christ died for our sins according to the Scriptures, and that He was buried, and that He was raised the **third day** *according to the Scriptures."* 1ˢᵗ *Corinthians 15:3-4*

"For as Jonah was three days and three nights in the belly of the great fish, so will the Son of Man be **three days and three nights** *in the heart of the earth."* *Matthew 12:40*

"Jewish Christians in the early church continued to celebrate the Passover, regarding Christ as the true Passover lamb. This naturally developed into a commemoration of the death and resurrection of our Lord because he was the true Passover sacrifice. But, while this Pascha or Passover celebration lasted three days, commemorating the death and resurrection of Jesus Christ, I must point out that this Passover celebration was a moveable celebration like Pentecost. It occurred on different days each year. There was NOT a "Good Friday" under this scheme! In fact, another encyclopedia stated this – prior to A.D. 325, Easter was variously celebrated on different days of the week, including Friday, Saturday, and Sunday. So, obviously there was no "Good Friday" before this time, because Easter could be celebrated on any day and from time to time, was celebrated on Friday."[1]

"All that changed in 325 A.D. when the Emperor Constantine convened the Council of Nicaea, which issued the Easter Rule, which states that Easter shall be celebrated on Sunday, but did not fix the particular Sunday. It was left to the Bishop of Alexandria to determine the exact Sunday, since that city was regarded as the authority in astrological matters. He was to communicate the results of his determination to other churches. But there was disagreement among the churches about doing it that way. It was not until the 7th century that the Easter matter was settled. Easter was to be on the first Sunday that occurred after the first full moon, on or after the vernal equinox. However, there is still a twist I need to mention here. The "full moon" in the rule is the ecclesiastical full moon, which is defined as the fourteenth day of a tabular lunation, where day one corresponds to the ecclesiastical New Moon. It does not always occur on the same date as the astronomical full moon."[2] "The ecclesiastical "vernal equinox" is always on March 21. Therefore, Easter must be celebrated on a Sunday between the dates of March 22 and April 25."[3]

Now while we can make the assumption that Jesus was in fact crucified on a Thursday we need to dig a little deeper into that. "While all cultures work on the basis of a 24-hour day, not all cultures begin and end their day at the same time. There are major differences in the Roman Day, the Jewish Day, and our Modern Day. The Roman Day began at 6:00 A.M. and closed at 6:00 A.M. the next morning. The Jewish Day began at sunset and closed at the next sunset (or from about 6:00 P.M. to the next 6:00 P.M.). Our Day begins at midnight and closes at midnight."[4]

Now that we have it cleared up that every day did not always start at midnight I am going to go on further and show you that it was likely that Jesus was crucified on a Thursday, but OUR Wednesday. Let's go over a piece of the Holy Scriptures to enlighten us on this subject.

"And it was the third hour, and they crucified Him." Mark 15:25

"And when the sixth hour had come, there was darkness over the whole land until the ninth hour. And at the ninth hour Jesus cried out with a loud voice, saying, Eloi, Eloi, lama sabachthani? which is translated, My God, My God, why have You forsaken Me?" Mark 15:33-34

"The context of this time delineation is Roman."[5] Thus the third hour would have been 9:00 A.M., which was the same time of the daily sacrifice of the morning. In Mark 15:33 we are told there was darkness over the whole land for three hours, starting at the sixth hour. This would have been from Noon until 3:00 P.M. "The evening sacrifice of the Jews took place at the 9th hour, 3:00 P.M. and was buried before sunset or about 6:00 P.M., which would be their Thursday and still our Wednesday."[6] "The Lord was taken down from the cross and placed in the tomb before sunset, before the beginning of the Sabbath."[7]

"Therefore, because it was the Preparation Day, that the bodies should not remain on the cross on the Sabbath (for that Sabbath was a high day), the Jews asked Pilate that their legs might be broken, and that they might be taken away." John 19:31

Here is where it gets somewhat confusing, but we have to deal with the normal weekly Sabbath and the High Sabbaths. "The parenthetical clause is the key to understanding the entire problem. What is true that a normal weekly Sabbath begins on sunset on Friday (about 6 p.m.), did you know that there are seven other "High Sabbaths," all but one of which are floating Sabbaths? By "floating Sabbaths," I mean they could occur on any day of the week. Therefore, there could have been two Sabbaths in one week, a high or floating Sabbath and a weekly Sabbath."[8] Here is an example of two Sabbaths in one week.

"Now it happened on the second Sabbath after the first that He went through the grainfields. And His disciples plucked the heads of grain and ate them, rubbing them in their hands." Luke 6:1

"In fact, Christ was crucified on the day before an High Sabbath (floating Sabbath), not the day before the normal Sabbath! Which high Sabbath was it? It was the first day of the Feast of Unleavened Bread, which was always held on the 15th of Nisan. The first day of the Feast of Unleavened Bread was an Holy Convocation or High Sabbath and though always on the 15th of Nisan, that High Sabbath might fall on any day of the week, depending on the year. And, do you know what the day before the Feast of Unleavened Bread was? PASSOVER (emphasis in original) Christ our Passover was sacrificed for us on the day of Passover!"[9]

Here are some verses about the Feast of Unleavened Bread:

"On the first day there shall be a holy convocation, and on the seventh day there shall be a holy convocation for you. No manner of work shall be done on them; except for each soul for eating; that only may be done by you." Exodus 12:16

"Six days shall work be done, but the seventh day is a Sabbath observance of rest, a holy convocation. You shall do no work; it is the Sabbath of Jehovah in all your dwellings. These are the set feasts of Jehovah, holy convocations, which you shall proclaim in their appointed seasons: On the fourteenth day of the first month at evening is the Passover unto Jehovah. And on the fifteenth day of the same month is the Feast of Unleavened Bread unto Jehovah; seven days you shall eat unleavened bread. On the first day you shall have a holy convocation; you shall do no labor of work." Leviticus 23:3-7

"And on the fifteenth day of this month is the feast; unleavened bread shall be eaten seven days." Numbers 28:17

Christ as the Passover sacrifice:

> *"Therefore purge out the old leaven, that you may be a new lump, even as you are unleavened. For indeed Christ, our Passover, was sacrificed for us."* 1st *Corinthians 5:7*

Finishing this up we will go to Matthew:

> *"Now after the Sabbath, as the first* **day of the week began to dawn***, Mary Magdalene and the other Mary came to see the tomb. And behold, there was a great earthquake; for an angel of the Lord descended from Heaven, and came and rolled back the stone from the door, and sat on it. His countenance was like lightning, and his clothing as white as snow. And the guards shook for fear of him, and became like dead men. And the angel answered and said to the women, Do not be afraid, for I know that you seek Jesus who was crucified. He is not here; for He is risen, as He said. Come, see the place where the Lord was lying."* *Matthew 28:1-6*

The first day of the week is Sunday. We know this because God had commanded Israel to remember the Sabbath (Saturday). For the Lord rested on the seventh day after He created the heavens and the earth. This is proof that Jesus did rise on a Sunday. One can debate whether Jesus was crucified on a Wednesday or Thursday but there can no longer be any debate as to whether it was a Friday. Good Friday doesn't make sense.

> *"Six days you shall labor and do all your work, and the seventh day is the Sabbath of Jehovah your God. In it you shall not do any work; you, nor your son, nor your daughter, nor your male servant, nor your female servant, nor your cattle, nor your sojourner who is within your gates. For in six days Jehovah made the heavens and the earth, the sea, and all that is in them, and rested the seventh day. Therefore Jehovah has blessed the Sabbath day and consecrated it."* *Exodus 20:9-11*

Chapter 5

Palm Sunday

Though much of this study has to do with the paganism that came about from the Roman Catholic Church we will not be dealing with Ash Wednesday, Lent, Fat Tuesday, etc. Ash Wednesday as well as Fat Tuesday are generally only celebrated by the RCC. This section will be discussing Palm Sunday. First let's take a look at Palm Sunday from a biblical aspect utilizing the Holy Scriptures.

"Rejoice greatly, O daughter of Zion! Shout, O daughter of Jerusalem! Behold, your King comes to you! He is righteous and having salvation, lowly, and riding on an ass, even on a colt, the foal of an ass." Zechariah 9:9

"The next day a great multitude that had come to the feast, when they heard that Jesus was coming to Jerusalem, took branches of palm trees and went out to meet Him, and cried out: Hosanna! Blessed is He who comes in the name of the Lord! The King of Israel!" John 12:12-13

"Then, six days before the Passover, Jesus came to Bethany, where Lazarus was, who had died, whom He raised from the dead." John 12:1

This states that the next day Jesus was coming to Jerusalem. Now we are going to take a look at the Romanized version of Palm Sunday. Palm Sunday is celebrated on the Sunday before Easter.

"Throughout the greater part of Europe, in defect of the palm tree, branches of some other tree, as box, yew, or willow, were blessed by the priests after mass, and distributed among the people, who forthwith carried them in a joyous procession, in memory of the Savior's triumphant entry into the holy city; after which they were usually burnt, and the ashes laid aside, to be sprinkled on the heads of the congregation on the ensuing Ash Wednesday, with the priest's blessing."[1] "In the extreme desire manifested under the ancient religion to realize all the particulars of Christ's passion, it was customary in some places to introduce into the procession a wooden figure of an ass, mounted on wheels, with a wooden human figure riding upon it, to represent the Saviour."[2] There are many more odd things that the RCC did (does) in regard to Palm Sunday a couple of more of which will be noted.

"Crosses of palm were made and blessed by the priests, and sold to the people as safeguards against disease."[3] "It was a saying that he who had not a palm in his hand on Palm Sunday, would have his hand cut off."[4] Now we will get into a bit of information regarding the RCC celebration of Palm Sunday.

"About nine on Palm Sunday morning, St. Peter's having received a great crowd of people, all in their best attire, one of the papal regiments enters, and forms a clear passage up to the central aisle. Shortly afterwards the 'noble guard,' as it is called, of the Pope – a superior body of men – takes its place, and the corps diplomatique and distinguished ecclesiastics arrive, all taking their respective seats in rows in the space behind the high altar, which is draped and fitted up with carpets for the occasion. The Pope's chief sacristan now brings in an armful of so-called palms, and place them on the altar."[5] "At 9:30 a burst of music is heard from the choir, the soldiers present arms, all are on the tiptoe of expectation, and a procession enters from a side chapel near the doorway. All eyes are turned in this direction, and the Pope is seen borne up the centre of the magnificent basilica in his sedia gestatoria. This chair of state is fixed on two long poles covered with red velvet, and the bearers are twelve officials, six before and six behind. They bear the ends of the poles on their shoulders, and walk so steadily as not to cause any uneasy motion. On this occasion, and always keeping in mind that the church is mourning, the Pope is plainly attired, and his mitre is white without ornament."[6] "Descending from his sedia gestatoria, his Holiness, after some intermediate ceremonies and singing, proceeds to bless the palms, which are brought to him from the altar. This blessing is effected by his reading certain prayers, and incensing the palms three times. An embroidered apron is now placed over the Pope's knees, and the cardinals in turn receive a palm from him, kissing the palm, his right hand, and knee. The bishops kiss the palm which they receive and his right knee; and the mitred abbots and other kiss the palm and his foot. Palms are now more freely distributed by sacristans, till at length, they reach those among the lay nobility who desire to have one. The ceremony concludes by reading additional prayers, and more particularly, by chanting and singing."[7] "In conclusion, low mass is performed by one of the bishops present, and the Pope, getting into his sedia gestatoria, is carried with the same gravity back to the chapel whence he issued, and which communicates with his residence in the Vatican. The entire ceremonial lasts about three hours, but many, to see it, endure the fatigue of standing five to six hours."[8]

As you can clearly see the celebration of Palm Sunday has nothing to do with the true Christian Church. This, like any other catholic mass, is not Christian at all. Rome is filled with pagan and superstitious practices that have invaded our churches and sadly been passed down and practiced by those who claim to know the Lord, and even those who truly do know the Lord. While the Lord may not have made one aware of this yet, it is the purpose of this study to allow those who are truly biblical Christians understanding and consider how they want to celebrate the Passover, Resurrection Sunday or whatever it may be that you call it.

Chapter 6

Easter

Out of the three parts to this study this will be the most eye-opening. This portion of the study will prove beyond a doubt that the origin of Easter is pagan. This is not to undermine the Christian remembering of the death and resurrection of our Lord and Savior Jesus Christ whatsoever. Please keep in mind that you will have to decide what you are going to do with this information on your own. You must consider the Holy Scriptures when doing so, of which I will include several verses throughout this study. Personally I have decided to call Easter, Resurrection Sunday and find it most fitting to celebrate it on the Jewish Passover.

"One person esteems one day above another; another esteems every day alike. Let each be fully assured in his own mind. He who regards the day, regards it to the Lord; and he who does not regard the day, to the Lord he does not regard it. He who eats, eats to the Lord, for he gives God thanks; and he who does not eat, to the Lord he does not eat, and gives God thanks." Romans 14:5-6

We are going to start off with a word study. The word we are going to be studying is Easter. According to my old Webster's dictionary:

Eas'ter, n., a paschal feast, originally a festival in honor of the Goddess of Spring, Eostre, held in April.[1]

This is the very first definition found in the dictionary and sheds some serious light on the Easter, henceforth 'Easter,' except while quoting.

'Easter' and the bible:

"And when he had apprehended him, he put him in prison, and delivered him to four quaternions of soldiers to keep him;

intending after Easter to bring him forth to the people." Acts 12:4 King James Version

"So when he had apprehended him, he put him in prison, and delivered him to four quaternions of soldiers to guard him, intending to bring him out to the people after Passover." Acts 12:4 VW-Edition (Source: www.a-voice.org)

Big difference here. The question will obviously arise, if 'Easter' is pagan then why is it in the KJV? I challenge you to grab a Strong's Concordance. Look up the word yourself and see that it is in fact Pascha or Passover. The word 'Easter' is NOT in the Holy Scriptures. It is not the purpose of this study to compare the KJV accuracy in terms of English translations, nor to demonize the KJV. I fully advocate the use of the KJV, but will not proclaim it to be without error or push KJV only. Personally I mostly use the VW-Edition of the Holy Scriptures, this error explained above being one of the reasons.

At this point we are going to thoroughly study 'Easter,' it's origins and the origins of the rituals that go along with it. We will begin by taking a look at some old reference books, regarding the origins of holidays (holy days), then moving on to some newer references, including a newer book and online resources.

Origins of the name 'Easter'

"Easter. The Sunday on which Christian Churches commemorate the resurrection of Christ. The name, which is in use only among the English and German speaking peoples, is derived, in all probability, from that of a goddess of the heathen Saxone, Ostara, Osterr, or Eastre. She was the personification of the East, of the morning, of the spring. The month of April was dedicated to her, and was called Eastermonath among the Saxons and Angles, and is still known in Germany as Ostermonat. Her worship struck deep root in Northern Germany, was carried to England by the Saxons, and still survives in some obscure customs in feasts to celebrate the return of the spring."[2]

"The name of the feast, according to the Venerable Bede, comes from Eostre, a Teutonic goddess whose festival was celebrated in the spring. Her name was given to the Christian festival in celebration of the Resurrection. Eostre it was who, according to the legend, opened the portals of Valhalla to receive Baldur, called the White God, because of his purity and also the Sun God, because his brow supplied light to mankind. It was Baldur who, after he had been murdered by Utgard Loki, the enemy of goodness and truth, spent half the year in Valhalla and the other half with the pale goddess of the lower regions."[3]

"The Teutonic name of the church feast of our Lord's resurrection. Bede gives as the name of fourth month, answering nearly to April, Eostremonath."[4]

"The first hint of something amiss is the word "Easter." Almost any resource material will cite a Teutonic goddess by a similar name, "Eostre" or "Eastre."

'Eostre was the deity of both the dawn and spring, and "the pagan symbol of fertility." At her festival in April, sacred fires were lighted on the hills, especially in the Nordic lands. (At this same season, ancient Romans observed the Feast of the Vernal Equinox.) - **Mamie R. Krythe, All About American Holidays, p. 98'**

Further investigation of this Teutonic name traces it back to Ostera, then Astarte, then to Ishtar (once pronounced as we do "Easter"). Since Ishtar, whose alternate name is Semiramis, was the wife of Nimrod, the priest and king of Babylon, we can trace a direct line between the word "Easter" and the origins of pagan religion.

"According to legend, when Nimrod died he proceeded to become the sun-god, while Semiramis (Easter) proceeded to have an illegitimate son, Tammuz, whom she claimed was the son of her deified Nimrod. She apparently claimed Tammuz was the promised seed of the woman (Gen. 3:15) and demanded worship for both herself as well as Tammuz. With only slight effort one can imagine that the mother soon was worshiped as much or more than her bastard son. Tammuz was later symbolized by a golden calf as the son of the sun-god, Nimrod (Ralph Woodrow, Babylon: Mystery Religion, pp. 9-10; Exodus 32:1-6). Moreover, when we discover where and how the blessed Mother originated, the plot both thickens and worsens!"[5]

"Furthermore, modern-day Easter falls right after the observance of the forty days of Lent. In ancient Babylon when Tammuz died, the followers of Semiramis joined her in mourning over the death of her son, Tammuz, for forty days."[6] "Some say that the name Easter comes from the name "Eostre" (the Saxon goddess), while others believe that it is derived from the name "Ishtar" or "Astarte" (the Assyrian counterpart for Semiramis). Nonetheless, it is quite evident that in both of these views the origin of the name Easter comes from a pagan deity that can easily be identifiable with the wife of Nimrod."[7]

"So He brought me to the door of the north gate of the house of Jehovah; and behold, women were sitting there weeping for Tammuz." Ezekiel 8:14

"Under the definition for Easter in Webster's Dictionary (College Edition) one finds: "originally the anem of pagan vernal festival...Eastre, dawn goddess." Further reading in an encyclopedia, or most books on the holidays will identify Eastre with the pagan goddess known variously as Eostre, Ishtar, Semeramis (sic), and Astarte. This is the same Babylonian "Queen of Heaven," whose worship is condemned in the Word of God."[8]

"The children gather wood, and the fathers kindle the fire, and the women knead dough, to make cakes to the Queen of Heaven and to pour out drink offerings to other gods, that they may provoke Me to anger." Jeremiah 7:18

"And all the men who knew that their wives had burned incense to other gods, and all the women who stood by, a great multitude, even all the people who lived in the land of Egypt, in Pathros, answered Jeremiah, saying, As for the Word that you have spoken to us in the name of Jehovah, we will not give heed to you. But we will prepare and do whatever goes forth out of our own

mouth, to burn incense to the Queen of Heaven, and to pour out drink offerings to her, as we have done, we, and our fathers, our kings, and our rulers, in the cities of Judah, and in the streets of Jerusalem. For then we had plenty of food, and were well-off, and saw no evil. But since we stopped burning incense to the Queen of Heaven and pouring out drink offerings to her, we have lacked everything, and have been consumed by the sword and by famine. And the women also said, when we burned incense to the Queen of Heaven, and poured out drink offerings to her, did we make our cakes in her image, and pour out drink offerings to her without our men? Then Jeremiah said to all the people, to the men and to the women, and to all the people who had given him that answer, saying: The incense that you burned in the cities of Judah, and in the streets of Jerusalem, you, and your fathers, your kings, and your rulers, and the people of the land; did not Jehovah remember them, and did it not come into His mind? Yes, so that Jehovah could no longer hold back because of the evil of your doings, because of the abominations which you have done! Therefore your land is a waste, and a wonder, and a curse, without inhabitant, as it is today. Because you have burned incense, and because you have sinned against Jehovah, and have not obeyed the voice of Jehovah, nor walked in His Law, nor in His statutes, nor did you walk in His testimonies, therefore this evil has happened to you, as it is this day. Moreover Jeremiah said to all the people and to all the women, Hear the Word of Jehovah, all Judah who are in the land of Egypt. Thus says Jehovah of Hosts, the God of Israel, saying: You and your wives have both spoken with your mouths, and fulfilled with your hands, saying, We will prepare and celebrate our vows that we have vowed, to burn incense to the Queen of Heaven, and to pour out drink offerings to her. You will arise and carry out your vows, and prepare and celebrate your vows. Therefore hear the Word of Jehovah, all Judah that lives in the land of Egypt: Behold, I have sworn by My great name, says Jehovah, that My name shall no more be named in the mouth of any man of Judah in all the land of Egypt, saying, The Lord Jehovah lives. Behold, I will watch over them for evil, and not for good. And all the men of Judah in the land of Egypt shall be consumed by the sword and by famine, until there is an end to them." Jeremiah 44:15-27

Including the definition in Webster's dictionary we have documented several references proving that the name 'Easter' is derived of pagan origin. There should be no doubt that the name 'Easter' is indeed pagan and should not be used by Christians.

How 'Easter's' Date Is Determined

"In the early Church Waster was identical in date with the Passover, as in fact the two festivals are identical in their root. But the opposition of the Christians to the Jews led to a change. The records of the Nicean Council of A.D. 325 show that this opposition was most acute. The very call for the Council breathed hostility against the Jews and those Christians who celebrated Easter on the day on which the Jews kept Passover. These Christians were called Quartodecimanians, because they celebrated Easter on the 14th day of Nisan, the first month of the Jewish year. But the opposition to the Quartodecimanians of Asia was more zealous than intelligent; for the artificial day chosen for Easter fell occasionally, as in 1805 and in 1825, on the 14th day of the Jewish Nisan, and the Christian Fathers, while bitterly opposed to the Jews, adopted without hesitation the Jewish mode of reckoning time by lunations. To make the matter worse, these lunations do not tally with the facts of astronomy. The result is that Easter calculations are so extraordinarily difficult as to lead to occasional mistakes, like that of 1818, when Easter was kept on the wrong day."[9]

"The Council of Nicaea in 325, decided that the celebration should occur on the same day throughout the church. It was finally decided that the date should be the Sunday after the first full moon following the spring equinox. The date for the equinox was fixed as March 21, and it was provided that if the full moon appeared on that date Easter should be the next Sunday. Consequently Easter moves between March 22 and April 25."[10]

In reference to the first quote regarding how 'Easter's' date is determined it should be noted that Christians should not hate their Jewish brothers and sisters, of course that which is quoted is the Roman Catholic Church, not the true Church. Though the Jews are in disbelief that Jesus was the Messiah, we do both believe in the

God of Abraham, Isaac, and Jacob. This point of hatred towards the Jews shows a satanic belief system that is passed down throughout the ages and amplified itself with Adolf Hitler, yet continues with the Arab counties to this day, as well as much anti-Semitism that is found all over the world. The Most High picked the Jewish people as His own and this is still true today. We Gentiles did not replace the Jews as many would believe. This study is not going to dwell further on this.

"I say then, have they stumbled that they should come to an end? Let it not be! But through their trespass, to provoke them to jealousy, salvation has come to the Gentiles." Romans 11:11

"For I am not ashamed of the gospel of Christ, for it is the power of God unto salvation to everyone who is believing, to the Jew first and also to the Greek." Romans 1:16

Origin of 'Easter' Eggs and the Bunny that Lays Them

There is candy all of the market in the form of eggs. You have Cadbury eggs, cartons of 'eggs', all sorts of candied eggs. Color packets are sold to color hard-boiled eggs before 'Easter'. Churches often participate in hiding eggs for children to find. Have you ever considered that bunnies do not lay eggs? Of course we know that eggs come from birds, particularly chickens, but how many people have ever considered why a bunny would be portrayed as having laid them? This section is going to focus on that as the 'Easter' bunny and eggs play the biggest role in many people's celebrations, including the White House. Let's take a look at the origin of these odd customs.

"As the legend continues, an egg of wondrous size fell from heaven one day and landed in the Euphrates River. Some equally wondrous fishes managed to roll the egg to shore, whereupon several doves descended from heaven and incubated the remarkable find. Soon, out popped Ishtar (or Semiramis), the goddess of Easter. The egg eventually became the universal symbol for fertility, and as such can be traced in pagan cultures worldwide."[11] "More significantly, both the egg and its hatchling predate the resurrection of Christ by more than two thousand years, eliminating any possible connection among eggs, Easter, and Jesus."[12]

"Eggs have become closely associated with Easter, and are regarded as a symbol of resurrection, for they hold the seeds of life, and represent the revival of fertility upon the earth. However, the egg as a life emblem is much older than Christianity."[13]

"Egg painting may have originated in Persia and Egypt centuries ago. When the custom migrated into Europe, possibly by way of the Knights of the Crusades, egg decorating became an elaborate art."[14]

"To be perfectly correct, it is the hare, not the rabbit, who should be honored as the most famous secular Easter symbol...Easter is a movable feast dependent for its date on the phase of the moon, and from antiquity the hare has been a symbol for the moon; the rabbit has not. Hares are born with their eyes open, rabbits are born blind; the Egyptian name for the hare was UN, meaning "open" or "to open," and the full moon watched open-eyed through out the night. According to legend, the hare was thought never to blink or close its eyes."[15]

"The egg also came to be regarded as symbolical of the resurrection, as it holds the seed of a new life. But eggs came to be associated with Easter originally because it was forbidden to eat them during Lent and on Easter Sunday they were served."[16] The egg, however, as a symbol of new life is much older than Christianity. And the coloring of it at the spring festival is also of very ancient origin. The Egyptians, the Persians, the Greeks, and the Romans used it in this way. Eggs were eaten during the spring festival from very early times."[17] "The children are told that the rabbit lays the Easter eggs and the eggs are sometimes hidden in the garden for the children to find. This is an adaptation on the pagan custom of regarding the rabbit as an emblem of fertility, that is, on new life."[18]

"The connections between Easter and the hare springs from the latter's connection with the moon. Easter, inasmuch as its date depends upon the moon, is in a sense a lunar holiday. Now, from very ancient times the hare has been a symbol for the moon. There are many reasons for this. A few only need to be given. The hare is a nocturnal animal, and comes out at night to feed. The females carries her young for a month, thus representing the lunar cycle. Both hare and moon were thought to have the power of changing their sex. The new moon was masculine, the waning moon feminine. The superstition about the hare is mentioned by Pliny, Archelaus, and others. It is crystallized in the lines of Beaumont and Fletcher:

'Hares that yearly sexes change,
Proteus, altering oft and strange,
Hecate with shapes three,
Let his maiden changed be.
Faithless Shepherdess, Act 111'"[19]

"The practice of using dyed eggs (Easter eggs) and buns (hot cross buns) during this festival was observed in certain pagan festivities of antiquity as well. In different ancient pagan rituals these items were offered up unto false gods. In China dyed or painted eggs are used during a sacred festivals, and the Druids of Britain used an egg as the sacred emblem of their order."[20]

So as you can see the bunny and the egg have nothing to do with Christianity. This is yet another 'christianized' pagan holiday that the RCC was behind. So while these things may be associated with Christian themes they are not Christian, but pagan. "With the rise of Puritanism in England and its abhorrence of religious ceremonial the Protestants for a long time took no notice of Easter, or any other of the church festivals."[21]

'Easter Lilies'

"The fragrant, waxy white flower we call the Easter lily is not a spring flower or an American flower at all. A lily growing on islands near Japan was taken to Bermuda and then traveled to the United States to become our most special Easter plant. Flower growers have learned how to make it bloom in time."[22]

"Having become symbolic of the season, churches worldwide decorate their altars with these beautiful flowers, and innumerable thousands of them are given away to women at Easter as gifts. Few, however, realize the ancient significance of such gifts! The so-called "Easter lily" has long been revered by pagans by various lands as a holy symbol associated with reproductive organs. It was considered a phallic symbol! One might easily surmise what was being suggested by sending a gift of such nature in ancient times."[23]

Sunrise Services

"Sunrise services are not unrelated to the Easter fires held on the tops of hills in continuation of the New Year fires, a worldwide observance in antiquity. Rites were performed at the vernal equinox welcoming the sun and its great power to bring new life to all growing things."[24]

"Speaking of 'sun' worship... I'm sure many readers will get riled up at this, like they do at X-mass time when I observe the total pagan nature of the tree with its lights. It has been 'most precious' to "Christians" throughout the years... the "Easter Sunrise Service". The "[c]hurch" celebrates it as a most sacred "Easter" service. 'Not going to rehash here the pagan-ness of "Easter", to the queen of heaven, Isis, Ashtoreth, Isthar, Eostre, etc. We have done that in the past, We celebrate the fulfillment of Passover/Firstfruits of Christ's Death and Resurrection."[25]

There are many more things that we could study but the purpose of this study is to allow the Christian to realize the pagan origins of 'Easter' and compare what the Holy Scriptures says about such thing, which we will now do.

"Do not be unequally yoked together with unbelievers. For what fellowship has righteousness with lawlessness? And what communion has light with darkness? And what agreement has Christ with Belial? Or what part has a believer with an unbeliever?"
2nd Corinthians 6:14-15

"Therefore God also gives them up to uncleanness, in the lusts of their hearts, to dishonor their bodies among themselves, who change the truth of God into the lie, and fear and serve the created things more than the Creator, who is blessed forever. Amen." Romans 1:24-25

"And even as they do not like to have God in their full *true knowledge, God gives them over to a reprobate mind, to do those things which are not fitting; being filled with every unrighteousness, sexual perversion, wickedness, covetousness, maliciousness; full of envy, murder, strife, deceit, depravity; whisperers, defamers, haters of God, insolent, proud, boasters, inventors of evil things, disobedient to parents, without understanding, untrustworthy, without natural affection, unforgiving, unmerciful; who, knowing the righteous judgment of God, that those who practice such things are deserving of death, not only do them, but also approve of those who practice them."* Romans 1:28-32

"Adulterers and adulteresses, do you not know that friendship with the world is enmity with God? Whoever therefore purposes to be a friend of the world is shown to be opposing God." Jacob 4:4

"Therefore, since we are the offspring of God, we ought not to think that the Divine is like gold or silver or stone, something engraved by art and man's devising. Truly, these times of ignorance God overlooked, but now commands all men everywhere to repent." Acts 17:29-30

"They have not known nor understood; for He has shut their eyes so that they cannot see; and their hearts so that they cannot understand. And no one considers within his heart, nor is there perception nor understanding to say, I have burned part of it in the fire; indeed, also I have baked bread on its coals; I have roasted flesh and eaten; and shall I make the rest of it into *an abomination? Shall I prostrate myself to a piece of wood? He feeds on ashes; a deceived heart has turned him aside, so that he cannot deliver his soul, nor say, Is this not a lie in my right hand?"* Isaiah 44:18-20

"Therefore Jehovah said, Whereas this people draw near with their mouth, and honor Me with their lips, but have removed their hearts far from Me, and their fear toward Me is taught by the commandment of men." Isaiah 29:13

"Or do you not know that as many of us as were immersed into Christ Jesus were immersed into His death? Therefore we were buried with Him through immersion into death, that just as Christ was raised from the dead by the glory of the Father, even so we also should walk in newness of life. For if we have been planted together in the likeness of His death, certainly we also shall be in resurrection, knowing this, that our old man was crucified with Him, that the body of sin might be nullified, that we should no longer serve sin." Romans 6:3-6

"and you are made full in Him, who is the Head of all rule and authority. In Him you were also circumcised with the circumcision made without hands, by putting off the body of the sins of the flesh, by the circumcision of Christ, buried with Him in immersion, in which you also were raised with Him through the faith of the working of God, who raised Him out from the dead." Colossians 2:10-12

Chapter 7

St. Valentine's Day

Let us take a brief look at another holiday (holy day). This time we are going to turn our attention to St. Valentine's Day. Perhaps others have grown out of this holiday and no longer celebrate. When I was in grade school we used to hand out Valentine's to several of the opposite sex. There was an exchange of little candy hearts with various sayings and heart shaped boxes of candy. In my youthful ignorance I never once considered the origins of such folly. For me it was just another holiday that I looked forward to. Which girl would give me a Valentine; my mother would get us kids a box of chocolates. However should a Christian celebrate St. Valentine's Day? Should they allow their children to celebrate it?

In this side study we are going to take a look at St. Valentine's Day from a historical perspective. We are going to use two sources that I obtained several years ago. The first will be from an old book, the second from an online source. Certainly there is much more information available online now than what there were several years ago, but this study is not meant to be in depth, rather just give you a basic overview.

Origins of St. Valentine's Day

"Now, there is no custom without a reason. But the reason for this cannot be found in the life of the good saint who is made to indorse the custom with his name. He wrote no love-songs. No one rises up to accuse him of casting sheep's eyes on any Roman maiden."[1] So if St. Valentine's was not responsible for originating this holiday then exactly who was he?

"He was a bishop or Pope of Rome who stood steadfast to the faith during the Claudian persecutions, and for that faith was cast into jail, where he cured his keeper's daughter of blindness."[2] Cupid is the centerpiece of St. Valentine's day, but did you also know that

Cupid is portrayed blind? "It is the pleasure of Cupid, blind himself, to bring upon his votaries a similar blindness, not to cure it."[3] As the story continues, "...the fate of St. Valentine when the miracle was made known to the authorities...*was*...they first beat him with clubs and then beheaded him."[4] Afterwards "what was left of him is preserved in the church of St. Praxedes at Rome, where a gate, now known as the Porta del Popolo, was formerly named, in his honor, Porta Valentini, or Valentine's Gate."[5] To quite the surprise there is yet another Catholic saint whom claims a share in the day. His name like the first was also St. Valentine.

St. Valentine, the second one, "...was the bishop who healed a son of Craton the rhetorician, and was choked to death bey (sic) a fish-bone."[6] Continuing, "either Valentine would be surprised to find himself a lovers' saint..."[7] So just where does St. Valentine's Day come from if neither of the Valentine's in the past have anything to do with the customs of today's holiday?

"Singing Cupids are thy choristers and thy precentors, and instead of the crosier the mystical arrow is borne before thee."[8]

According to an etymologist "v and g were frequently interchangeable in popular speech, and as a notable instance produces the words gallant and valiant, which both spring from the Latin valens. He then explains that the Norman work galantine, a lover of the fair sex, or what in these slangy days might be called a masher, was frequently written and pronounced valantan or valentine. And from these premises he concludes that by a natural confusion of names Bishop Valentine was established as the patron saint of sweethearts and lovers, although he has no real connection, not even an etymological one, with that class of beings."[9] While this can certainly explain how St. Valentine came to be associated with the holiday, it does not explain the origin of the customs. There is more to the story and for that we turn to a lexicographer.

Looking at the first of the great English dictionaries, we will source Bailey from 1721. "Valentines (in England). About this time of the year – month of February – the Birds choose their Mates, and probably thence came the Custom of the Young Men and Maidens choosing Valentines, or special loving Friends, on that Day."[10] This is still not a good explanation so we will now turn to the antiquary, Francis Douce in his *Illustrations of Shakespeare*, 1807.

Douce 'suggests that St. Valentine's Day is the Christianized form of the classic Lupercalia, which were feasts held in Rome during the month of February in honor of Pan and Juno (hence known as Juno Februata", when amoung other ceremonies it was customary to put the names of young women into a box, from which they were drawn by the men as chance directed, and that the Christian clergy, finding it difficult or impossible to extirpate the pagan practice, gave it at least a religious aspect by substituting the names of particular saints for those of the women."[11] His claim is backed up by Rev. Alban Butler, a hagiologist. *(...the author of a worshipful or idealizing biography)*[12]

According to the book, *Lives of the Saints*, Butler explains that "pastors of the Christian Church, 'by every means in their power, worked zealously to readicate the vestiges of pagan superstition; chiefly by the simple process of retaining the ceremonies, but modifying their significance; and substituted, for the drawing of names in honor of the goddess Febrata Juno, the names of some particular saints. But as the festival of the Lupercalia took place during February, the 14 of that month, St. Valentine's Day, was selected for this new feast, as occurring about the same time."[13] To further evaluate the origin of this holiday we turn to John Lydgate and a poem in praise of Catherine, the wife of Henry V.

> *Seynte Valentine of custome yeere by yeere*
> *Men have an usuance, in this regioun,*
> *To love and serche Cupides kalendere,*
> *And chose theyr choyse by grete affeccioun,*
> *Such as ben move with Cupides mocioun,*
> *Takyng theyre choyse as theyre sort doth falle;*
> *But I love oon whiche excelleth alle.*[14]
> *(Fourteenth Century)*

Turning to a more modern day source we gather the following information, "in the days of the Roman Empire, the month of February was the last and shortest month of the year. February originally had 30 days, but when Julius Caesar named the month of July after himself, he decided to make that month longer and shortened February to 29 days while making July a month of 31 days. Later when Octavius Caesar, also known as Augustus, came to power, he named the month of August after himself, and not be outdone he also subtracted a day from February and gave the month of August 31 days. To this very day it remains that way. The ancient Romans believed that every month had a spirit that gained in strength and reached its peak or apex of power in the middle or ides of the month. This was usually the 15th day, and it was a day when witches and augurs, or soothsayers worked their magic. An augur was a person filled with a spirit of divination, and from the word augur we get the word "inaugurate", which means to "take omens". Since February had been robbed by Caesars and had only 28 days, the ides of February became the 14th day of that month. Since the Ides of a month was celebrated on the preceding eve, the month of February was unique, because it was the 13th day that became the eve of the Ides that month, and it became a very important pagan holiday in the Empire of Rome. The sacred day of February 14th was called "Lupercalia" or "day of the wolf." This was a day that was sacred to the sexual frenzy of the goddess Juno. This day also honored the Roman gods, Lupercus and Faunus, as well as the legendary twin brothers, who supposedly founded Rome, Remus and Romulus. These two are said to have been suckled by wolves in a cave on Palatine Hill in Rome. The cave was called Lupercal and was the center of the celebrating on the eve of Lupercalia or February 14th. On this day, Lupercalia, which was later named Valentine's Day, the Luperci or priests of Lupercus dressed in goatskins for a bloody ceremony. The priests of Lupercus, the wolf god, would sacrifice goats and a dog and then smear themselves with blood. These priests, made red with sacrificial blood, would run around Palatine Hill in a wild frenzy while carving a goatskin thong called a "februa." Women would sit all around the hill, as the bloody priests would strike them with the goatskin thongs to make them fertile. The young women would then gather in the city and their names were put in boxes. These "love notes" were called "billets." The men of Rome would draw a billet, and the woman whose name was on it became his sexual lust partner with whom he would fornicate until the next Lupercalia or February 14th."[15]

This concludes our brief look at the origin of St. Valentine's Day. As a Christian you will have to decide what to do with this information.

"And if it seems evil to you to serve Jehovah, choose for yourselves this day whom you will serve, whether the gods which your fathers have served that were on the other side of the River, or the gods of the Amorites, in whose land you are living. But as for me and my house, we will serve Jehovah." Joshua 24:15

Chapter 8

Christmas

The bible study supplement is going to look into the common customs, rituals and traditions that are associated with the Christ 'mass' holiday (holy day). We also will focus on the origins of the pagan tree that adorns homes all over America and most of the world every winter solstice celebration. This study will be utilizing several sources both that are from historical books as well as available on the internet.

A Savior is born...

"For there is born to you this day in the city of David a Savior, who is Christ the Lord." Luke 2:11

Yes indeed! Our Savior was born and He fulfilled prophecy, He was born in Bethlehem (*Matt. 2:1*) and His life, God's gift to mankind made our Salvation possible. His death on the cross paid the penalties for our sin. He is the hope of every Christian.

"Now may the God of hope fill you with all joy and peace in believing, that you may abound in hope by the power of the Holy Spirit." Romans 15:13

Should Christians celebrate Jesus's birthday?

The question must be presented, why do we celebrate the birth of Jesus Christ on a specific day? Should His birth, life, death and Resurrection not be celebrated every day in a Christian's life? Are birthdays celebrated in the bible?

"And it came to pass on the third day, which was Pharaoh's birthday, that he made a feast for all his servants; and he lifted up the head of the chief cupbearer and of the chief baker among his servants." Genesis 40:20

"Then an opportune day came when Herod on his birthday made a feast for his nobles, the high officers, and the chief men of Galilee." Mark 6:21

These are the only two birthdays being celebrated that are mentioned in God's Word. Both of these men who celebrated their birthdays were pagan leaders of the people. If God wanted us to set aside a day each year to celebrate the birth of His Son Jesus, would not a date have been clearly given? Why is it that the bible is silent on the date of Jesus's birth? We will be discussing the origin of December 25th having been selected as the day that the world's Christians set aside to celebrate the birth of Jesus later. First we are going to take a look at which season Jesus could not have been born in.

Was Jesus born on December 25th?

While the Holy Scriptures are silent on the date of Jesus's birth we can determine that Jesus could not have been born in the month of December by using Scripture.

"Now there were in the same country shepherds living out in the fields, keeping watch over their flock by night." Luke 2:8

"Bethlehem has a Mediterranean climate, with hot and dry summers and cold winters. Temperatures in the winter season, from mid-December to mid-March, could be cold and rainy. January is the coldest month, with temperatures ranging from 1 to 13 degree Celsius (33–55 °F). From May through September, the weather is warm and sunny. August is the hottest month, with a high of 27 degrees Celsius (81 °F). Bethlehem receives an average of 700 millimeters (27.6 in) of rainfall annually, 70% between November and January."[1]

"**Keeping watch - by night** - Or, as in the margin, keeping the watches of the night, i.e. each one keeping a watch (which ordinarily consisted of three hours) in his turn. The reason why they watched them in the field appears to have been, either to preserve the sheep from beasts of prey, such as wolves, foxes, etc., or from

41

freebooting banditti, with which all the land of Judea was at that time much infested. It was a custom among the Jews to send out their sheep to the deserts, about the Passover, and bring them home at the commencement of the first rain: during the time they were out, the shepherds watched them night and day. As the Passover occurred in the spring, and the first rain began early in the month of Marchesvan, which answers to part of our October and November, we find that the sheep were kept out in the open country during the whole of the summer. And as these shepherds had not yet brought home their flocks, it is a presumptive argument that October had not yet commenced, and that, consequently, our Lord was not born on the 25th of December, when no flocks were out in the fields; nor could he have been born later than September, as the flocks were still in the fields by night. On this very ground the nativity in December should be given up. The feeding of the flocks by night in the fields is a chronological fact, which casts considerable light upon this disputed point."[2]

A very good argument has been made as to why Jesus couldn't have been born in December. We are going to take a look at another argument against December based off of the Holy Scriptures.

"And it came to pass in those days that a decree went out from Caesar Augustus that all the world should be registered. This census first took place while Cyrenius was governing Syria. So all went to be registered, everyone to his own city. Joseph also went up from Galilee, out of the city of Nazareth, into Judea, to the city of David, which is called Bethlehem, because he was of the house and lineage of David, to be registered with Mary, his betrothed wife, who was with child. So it was, that while they were there, the days were fulfilled for her to give birth. And she gave birth to her firstborn Son, and wrapped Him in swaddling cloths, and laid Him in a manger, because there was no room for them in the inn." Luke 2:1-7

The thought being here is that a census would not be taken during the cold winter months, but rather during more favorable weather, either spring, summer or early fall. While this can not seemingly be proven, as history is often distorted by those who write it and varying contradictions can appear out of alternative historical works, this is a common sense argument. Once the origin of the selecting of December 25th is investigated this theory will become even more grounded.

Origin of December 25th, Jesus's birthday or an ancient pagan holy day?

Now we will divulge the origin of Christ 'mass' and see how indeed this date was well-known and celebrated long before the birth of Christ. We will also look into how it became associated with Jesus's birth. Here is an excerpt from an old book regarding the origin of Christ 'mass'.

"This festival has been commonly believed to have had only an astronomical character, referring simply to the completion of the sun's yearly course, and the commencement of a new cycle. But there is indubitable evidence that the festival in question had a much higher influence than this--that it commemorated not merely the figurative birthday of the sun in the renewal of its course, but the birth-day of the grand Deliverer...the Sun-God and great mediatorial divinity."[3]

Here we can see that early Christians did not celebrate Christ 'mass', as pointed out in the study regarding the origin of the tree the holiday was banned in the mid 1600's in Massachusetts Bay Colony.

"...within the Christian Church no such festival as Christmas was ever heard of till the third century, and...not till the fourth century was far advanced did it gain much observance. How, then, did the Romish Church fix on December 25th as Christmas-day? Why, thus: Long before the fourth century, and long before the Christian era itself, a festival was celebrated among the heathen, at that precise time of the year, in honour of the birth of the son of the Babylonian queen of heaven; and it may fairly be presumed that, in order to conciliate the heathen, and to swell the number of nominal adherents of Christianity, the same festival was adopted by the Roman Church, giving it the name of Christ."[4]

Probably one of the main reasons that many so-called Christians would have a very hard time seeing through the matter, though if they are not truly saved they ought to focus on that first and foremost!, is the fact that there is so much ecumenism. Not all who call themselves Christians are indeed truly saved and not all of the Churches are truly New Testament Churches that are honorable and obedient to the Most High.

"For not all those of Israel are Israel." Romans 9:6b

The study is written for Christians or for whomever God desires to read it. The 'christian' world can not readily mark off their Catholic brethren, the root of so-called christianizing of this pagan holiday. With the amount of ecumenism, one-ness, agreeing to disagree – but keeping the basics, or whatever title such stuff goes under it is no wonder that biblical Christianity is indeed something found by only the few.

"Because narrow is the gate and distressing is the way which leads unto life, and there are few who find it." Matthew 7:14

Here is the origin of attaching Jesus's day of birth to December 25th.

"Many Roman Catholics would like to point to Pope Liberius, who in 354 A.D. decreed Christmas to be celebrated December 25th. In reality it was the Roman Emperor, Constantine who declared December 25th to be Christ's birthday in the year 336 A.D. What was his reason for this? It was based on political pressure! Many zealous church members urged the decree.

Why December 25th? That day was already observed as a heathen holiday...'THE FEAST OF SATURN, BIRTHDAY OF THE UNCONQUERED SUN.' This pagan feast began two weeks of festivities which included feasting, drinking, abstention from work, special musical presentations and the exchanging of gifts.

You will remember that Constantine was the first 'christian' emperor of the Roman Empire. As a result of a vision of the cross, (inscribed with "in hoc signo vinces" which in Latin means – by this emblem shalt thou conquer) in 312 A.D. Constantine gave full support to Christianity and proclaimed it the official religion of the Empire."[5]

In order to put this matter to rest regarding the historical truths of December 25th and the winter solstice we are going to briefly review a snippet about the dating of the winter solstice and then go over some historical documentation regarding Christ 'mass' and the origins.

"Since 45 BCE, when the 25th of December was established in the Julian calendar as the winter solstice of Europe, (Latin: *Bruma*), the difference between the calendar year (365.2500 days) and the tropical year (365.2422 days) moved the day associated with the actual astronomical solstice forward approximately three days every four centuries until 1582 when Pope Gregory XIII changed the calendar bringing the northern winter solstice to around December 21. Yearly, in the Gregorian calendar, the solstice still fluctuates slightly but, in the long term, only about one day every 3000 years."[6]

Here we can see that the winter solstice was celebrated on December 25th. Now moving right along...

Historical Documentation

"In pagan Rome and Greece, in the days of the Teutonic barbarians, in the remote times of ancient Egyptian civilization, in the infancy of the race East and West and North and South, the period of the winter solstice was ever a period of rejoicing and festivity. Even the Puritanism of the Anglo-Saxon has not been equal to the task of defending Yule-tide from a triumphant inroad of pagan rites and customs..."[7]

"The wild revels, indeed, of the Christmas period in olden times almost stagger belief. Obscenity, drunkenness, blasphemy, --

nothing came amiss. License was carried to the fullest extent of the licentiousness."[10]

"Merrie (sic) old England was the soil in which Merrie Christmas took its firmest root. Even in Anglo-Saxon days we hear of Alfred holding high revelry in December, 878, so that he allowed the Danes to surprise him, cut his army to pieces, and send him a fugitive. The court revelries increased in splendor after the Conquest. Christmas, it must be remembered, was not then a single day of sport. It had its preliminary novena which began December 16, and it ended on January 6, or Twelfth-Night. All this period was devoted to holiday-making."[11]

"We have frequently…had occasion to remark on the numerous traces still visible in popular customs of the old pagan rites and ceremonies. There, it is needless here to repeat, were extensively retained after the conversion of Britain to Christianity, partly because the Christian teachers found it impossible to wean their converts from their cherished superstitions and observances, and partly because they themselves, as a matter of expediency, ingrafted the rites of the Christian religion on the old heathen ceremonies, believing that thereby the cause of the Cross would be rendered more acceptable to the generality of the populace, and thus be more effectually promoted."[14]

Taking a moment aside to mention just how telling this really is. Understandably much European literature, as the above, was written by Catholics or those who only saw the Catholic faith as the sole means of Christianity. So much of history dealing with Christianity has a very heavy or predominant Catholic slant. The above is quite telling as it is not only what is happening today with the churches who will have rock concerts, other worldly sponsorships and events as well as their 'come-as-you-are' type settings to even relates it to the fact that the teachers or proselytizers themselves were unwilling to give up worldly things for the cause of Christ.

"Do not be unequally yoked together with unbelievers. For what fellowship has righteousness with lawlessness? And what

communion has light with darkness? And what agreement has Christ with Belial? Or what part has a believer with an unbeliever? And what agreement has the temple of God with idols? For you are the temple of the living God. As God has said: I will dwell in them and walk among them. I will be their God, and they shall be My people. Therefore, Come out from among them and be separate, says the Lord. Do not touch what is unclean, and I will receive you." 2nd Corinthians 6:14-17*

"But Jesus said to him, No one, having put his hand to the plow, and looking back, is fit for the kingdom of God." Luke 9:62

As if that were not telling enough it gets even more obvious. In fact this historical source simply explains it as it is...

"In the early ages of Christianity, its ministers frequently experienced the utmost difficulty in inducing the converts to refrain from indulging in the popular amusements which were so largely participated in by their pagan countrymen. Among others, the revelry and licence (sic) which characterized the Saturnalia called for special animadversion. But at last, convinced partly of the inefficacy of such denunciations, and partly influenced by the idea that the spread of Christianity might thereby be advanced, the church endeavored to amalgamate, as it were, the old and new religions, and sought, by transferring the heathen ceremonies to the solemnities of the Christian festivals, to make them subservient to the cause of religion and piety. A compromise was thus effected between clergy and laity, though it must be admitted that it proved anything but a harmonious one, as we find a constant, though ineffectual, proscription by the ecclesiastical authorities of the favourite amusements of the people, including among others the sports and revelries at Christmas.

Engrafted thus on the Roman Saturnalia, the Christmas festivities received in Britain further changes and modifications, by having superadded to them, first, the Druidical rites and superstitions, and then, after the arrival of the Saxons, the various ceremonies practiced by the ancient Germans and Scandinavians. The result has been the strange medley of Christian and pagan rites which contribute to make up the festivities of the modern Christmas."[19]

Continuing on a historical aspect of the origins…

"…the festivities of which, originally derived from the Roman Saturnalia, had afterwards been intermingled with the ceremonies observed by the British Druids at the period of the winter-solstice, and at a subsequent period became incorporated with the grim mythology of the ancient Saxons."[15]

"Sir Isaac Newton, indeed, remarks in his *Commentary of the Prophecies of Daniel*, that the feast of the Nativity, and most of the other ecclesiastical anniversaries, were originally fixed at cardinal points of the year, without any reference to the dates of the incidents which they commemorated, dates which, by the elapse of time, had become impossible to be ascertained. Thus the Annunciation of the Virgin Mary was placed on the 25th of March, or about the time of the vernal equinox; the feast of St. Michael on the 29th of September, or near the autumnal equinox; and the birth of Christ and other festivals at the time of the winter-solstice. Many of the apostles' days – such as St. Paul, St. Matthias, and others – were determined by the days when the sun entered the respective signs of the ecliptic, and the pagan festivals had also a considerable share in the adjustment of the Christian year…Though Christian nations have thus, from an early period in the history of the church, celebrated Christmas about the period of the winter-solstice or the shortest day, it is well known that many, and, indeed, the greater number of the popular festive observances by which it is characterized, are referrible (sic) to a much more ancient origins. Amid all the pagan nations of antiquity, there seems to have been a universal tendency to worship the sun as the giver of life and light, and the visible manifestation of the Deity. Various as were the names bestowed by different peoples on this object of their worship, he was still the same divinity. Thus, at Rome, he appears to have been worshipped under one of the characters attributed to Saturn, the father of the gods; among the Scandinavian nations he was known under the epithet of Odin or Woden, the father of Thor, who seems afterwards to have shared with his parent the adoration bestowed on the latter, as the divinity of which the sun was the visible manifestation; whilst with the ancient Persians, the appellation for the god of light was Mithras, apparently the same as the Irish Mithr, and with the Phoenicians or Carthaginians it was Baal or Bel, an epithet familiar to all students of the Bible."[17]

"Others have derived it from some one or other of the Roman festivals held in the latter part of December, as the Saturnalia, or the Sigillaria which followed them, or the Juvenalia established by Nero. A more striking parallel, however, than any of these is to be found in the Brumalia, or the Natalis Invicti (Solis), when the Sun, then at the winter solstice, was, as it were, born anew...Mr. King (Gnostics and their Remains, p. 49), who derives the Roman festival from the Mithras-worship of the Sun. Then as Mithraicism gradually blended with Christianity, changing its name but not altogether its substance, many of its ancient notions and rites passed over too, and the Birthday of the Sun, the visible manifestation of Mithras himself, was transferred to the commemoration of the Birth of Christ."[22]

"In the West it (Christmas) has been celebrated on 25 Dec since 336 AD, partly in order to replace the non-Christian sun worship on the same date."[28]

Customs, Rituals and Traditions

Now that we have taken an exhausting look into the roots of Christ 'mass' it should be more than suffice for even the hardest skeptic to acknowledge that the Lord Jesus Christ and the celebration of Christ 'mass' have nothing in common. Let's turn our attention to some of the other customs, rituals and traditions that go along with the celebration of this pagan holiday and see that despite common misconceptions the true origins of these things are indeed pagan.

Holly and Mistletoe

"Yet the holly and the mistletoe are a survival of ancient Druidical worship..."[8]

"Two popular observances belonging to Christmas are more especially derived from the worship of our pagan ancestors – the hanging up of the mistletoes, and the burning of the Yule long. As regards the former of these practices, it is well known that, in the religion of the Druids, the mistletoe was regarded with the utmost veneration, though the reverence which they paid to it seems to have been restricted to the plant when found growing on the oak – the favourite tree of their divinity Tutanes – who appears to have been the same as the Phenician (sic) god Baal, or the sun, worshipped under so many different names by the various pagan nations of antiquity. At the period of the winter-solstice, a great festival was celebrated in his honour, as will be found more largely commented on under our notice of Christmas Day. When the sacred anniversary arrived, the ancient Britons, the sylvan deities during the season of frost and cold. These rites in connection with the mistletoe, were retained throughout the Roman dominion in Britain, and also for a long period under the sovereignty of the Jutes, Saxons, and Angles.

The following legend regarding the mistletoe, from the Scandinavian mythology, may here be introduced: Balder, the god of poetry and eloquence, and second son of Odin and Friga, communicated one day to his mother a dream which he had had, intimating that he should die. She (Friga), to protect her son from such a contingency, invoked all the powers of nature – fire, air, earth, and water, as well as animals and plants – and obtained an oath from them that they should do Balder no hurt. The latter then went and took his place amid the combats of the gods, and fought accompanied by their priests, the Druids, sallied forth with great pomp and rejoicing to gather the mystic parasite, which, in addition to the religious reverence with which it was regarded, was believed to posses wondrous curative powers. When the oak was reached on which the mistletoe grew, two white bulls were bound to the tree and the chief Druid, clothed in white (the emblem of purity), ascended, and, with a golden knife, cut the sacred plant, which was caught by another priest in the folds of his robe. The bulls, and often also human victims, were then sacrificed, and various festivities followed. The mistletoe thus gathered, was divided into small portions, and distributed among the people, who hung up the sprays over the entrances to their dwellings, as a propitiation and shelter to without fear in the midst of showers of arrows, Loake, his enemy, resolved to discover the secret of Balder's invulnerability, and, accordingly, disguising himself as an old woman, he addressed himself to Friga with complimentary remarks on the valour and good-fortune of her son. The goddess replied that no substance could injure him, as all the productions of nature had bound themselves by an oath to refrain from doing him any harm. She added, however, with the awkward simplicity which appears so often to characterize mythical personages, that there was one plant which, from its insignificance, she did not think of conjuring, as it was impossible that it could inflict any hurt on her son. Loake inquired the name of the plant in question, and was informed that it was a feeble little shoot, towing on the bark of the oak, with scarcely any soil. Then the treacherous Loake ran and procured the mistletoe, and, having entered the assembly of the gods, said to the blind Heda: 'Why do you not contend with the arrows of Balder?' Heda replied: 'I am blind, and have no arms.' Loake then presented him with an arrow formed from the mistletoe, and said: 'Balder is before thee,' Heda shot, and Balder fell pierced and slain."[16]

Christ 'mass' Carols

"...the Christmas carol is a new birth, purified and exalted, of the hymns of the Saturnalia..."[9]

"The Puritans, indeed, denounced not only the singing of Christmas carols, but the observance of the festival of Christmas itself, as pernicious an unscriptural, and to their influence has been ascribed much of the seriousness characterizing this department of popular poetry in later times."[20]

Christ 'mass' Lights and Candles

"Throughout Northern Germany the tables are spread and light left burning during the entire night, that the Virgin Mary and the angel who passes when everybody sleeps many find something to eat. In certain parts of Austria they put candles in the windows, that the Christ-Child may not stumble in passing through the village."[12]

"An Arab geographer quoted in the tenth century a tradition that trees and flowers blossomed on Christmas and in the thirteenth century a French epic tells of candles appearing of the flowering trees."[25]

"The candles were lighted by the pagans on the eve of the festival of the Babylonian god, to do honor to him, for it was one of the distinguishing peculiarities of his worship to light wax candles on his altars."[30]

Presents

"A similar custom prevailed among the Romans (giving of gifts),...on the Calends of January offered to the emperor or their patrons presents called strenae...the custom of the strenae as an offshoot of heathenism, did not find much favour in the eyes of the early Church."[23]

"The giving of presents on January 1 by the Romans has survived as the giving of Christmas remembrances, or as it is sometimes called the exchange of presents." [24]

Miscellaneous Christ 'mass' Decorations

"The use of wreaths at Christmas time is believed by authorities to be traceable to the pagan customs of decorating building and places of worship at the feast of the winter solstice."[29]

Note: Common sense after completing this study would seem to point to wreaths representing the sun, or worship of the sun.

"The custom of decorating the houses with greens is derived from...(the) belief in the blossoming of trees and plants at Christmas. Yet one archbishop forbade the use of greens on the assumption that the custom was of heathen origin. The use of mistletoe is without doubt traced to the Druids, who regarded it with reverence long before the Christian era. In celebration of the winter solstice the Druid priests gathered mistletoe and piled it on the altar of their god and burned it in sacrifice to him...whenever enemies met under the mistletoe they would drop their arms, forget their enmities and embrace. It is believed that the custom of kissing under the mistletoe grew out of this ancient practice."[25]

"The decking of churches, houses, and shops with evergreens at Christmas, springs from a period far anterior to the revelation of Christianity, and seems proximately to be derived from the custom prevalent during the Saturnalia of the inhabitants of Rome ornamenting their temples and dwelling with green boughs. From this latter circumstance, we find several early ecclesiastical councils prohibiting the members of the church to imitate the pagans in thus ornamenting their houses. But in process of time, the pagan custom was like others of a similar origin, introduced into and incorporated with the ceremonies of the church itself."[21]

The winter-solstice "by the Romans, this anniversary was celebrated under the title of Saturnalia, or the festival of Saturn, and was marked by the prevalence of a universal license and merry-making. The slaves were permitted to enjoy for a time a thorough freedom in speech and behaviour, and it is even said that their masters waited on them as servants. Every one feasted and rejoiced, work and business were for a season entirely suspended, the houses were decked with laurels and evergreens, presents were made by parents and friends, and all sorts of games and amusements were indulged in by the citizens. In the bleak north, the same rejoicing had place, but in a ruder and more barbarous form. Fires were extensively kindled, both in and out of doors, blocks of wood blazed in honour of Odin and Thor, the sacred mistletoe was gathered by the Druids, and sacrifices, both of men and cattle, were made to the savage divinities. Fires are said, also, to have been kindled at this period of the year by the ancient Persians, between whom and the Druids of Western Europe a relationship is supposed to have existed."[18]

"In Germany the decoration of the house begins as early as the morning of the 24th. One room, from which all save "die Mutter" is rigidly excluded, contains the Christmas-tree and all the presents, set in a shining row upon the table. Greens are hung from window and door, and garlands upon the walls…The children's eyes are glued to the sliding doors, which are presently to open and disclose the tree. Six o'clock, -- a bell rings. Back swings the portal, and there it stands, resplendent with lights and tinsel."[13]

"The sin of Judah is written with an iron stylus; it is engraved on the tablet of the heart and on the horns of Your altar with the point of a diamond; while their children remember their altars and their groves by the green trees on the high hills. O My mountain in the field, I will give your wealth and all your treasures for plunder, and your high places for sin, throughout all your borders. And you, even yourself, have let go of the inheritance which I gave you; and I will cause you to serve your enemies in a land which you do not know. For you have kindled a fire in My anger, which shall burn forever. Thus says Jehovah, Cursed is the man who trusts in man, and makes flesh his strength, and whose heart departs from Jehovah." Jeremiah 7:1-5

Another tidbit on the Puritans...

"There was a time during the Puritan ascendancy in England when the observance of Christmas was forbidden. A law was passed in 1644 making December 25 a market day and ordering that the shops be kept open. The making of plum puddings and mince pies was forbidden as a heathen custom. This law was repealed after the Restoration, but the Dissenters ridiculed the celebration of Christmas by calling it "Fooltide" in burlesque of Yuletide. The General Court of Massachusetts passed a law in 1659 making the observance of Christmas a penal offense. This law was later repealed as the English law had been, but it was many years before there were any general Christmas celebrations in New England."[26]

A Final Thought

While it is clear that Christ 'mass' has been celebrated for well over a millennia it should be noted that time does not make evil not evil or sin not sin. Some of the things that we are used to in America are not as old as they seem. Here is a great example:

"Early in the present century the custom of setting up a Christmas tree in a public place and decorating it with colored lights was adopted in many American cities. In 1909 the people of Pasadena, Calif., instead of setting up a tree in the city, selected a tall evergreen on Mount Wilson, decorated it with lights and tinsel and loaded it with gifts which were distributed on Christmas day. In 1912 a tree was set up in Madison Square in New York and on the Common in Boston for the first time. And in 1914 a tree was placed in Independence Square in Philadelphia."[27]

So you see what we perceive to having always been done in fact hasn't hardly been done a hundred years, in many cases several years less than that.

What then should a Christian do in regards to this information? Should a Christian still celebrate Christ 'mass' or not? What about ones friends and family, what will they think?

The Most High hates idolatry and this is what Christ 'mass' is all about. Christians should not partake of the Catholic mass, which is the origin of the name of this pagan holiday.

"Therefore, my beloved, flee from idolatry." 1st Corinthians 10:14

"You shall have no other gods before Me. You shall not make for yourself a carved image; any likeness of anything in the heavens above, or in the earth beneath, or in the waters under the earth; you shall not bow down to them nor serve them; for I, Jehovah your God, am a jealous Mighty God, visiting the iniquity of the fathers upon the sons to the third and fourth generations of those who hate Me, but showing mercy to thousands, to those who love Me and keep My commandments." Deuteronomy 5:7-10

We are called by God to live holy and righteous lives before Him. We are to be separate from the world. What the world does in celebrating Christ 'mass' is not for us. Just as rock music has crept into many churches around the country we mustn't dismiss this error just because it is far older.

"Just as He chose us in Him before the foundation of the world, that we should be holy and without blemish before Him in love." Ephesians 1:4

"And you, who once were alienated and hostile in your mind by wicked works, yet now He has reconciled in the body of His flesh through death, to present you holy, and without blemish, and above reproach in His sight." Colossians 1:21-22

"Therefore gird up the loins of your mind, be sober, and rest your hope fully upon the grace that is to be brought to you at the revelation of Jesus Christ; as obedient children, not conforming yourselves to the former lusts in your ignorance; but as He who called you is holy, you also become holy in all conduct, because it is written, Be holy, because I am holy." 1st Peter 1:13-16

"If you know that He is righteous, you know that everyone who produces righteousness is born of Him." 1st John 2:29

"For the righteous Jehovah loves righteousness; His face beholds the upright." Psalms 11:7

"The righteous shall inherit the earth, and dwell in it forever." Psalms 37:29

"And do not be conformed to this world, but be transformed by the renewing of your mind, that you may prove what is that good and acceptable and perfect will of God." Romans 12:2

"Do not love the world or the things in the world. If anyone loves the world, the love of the Father is not in him." 1st John 2:15

"Come out of her, my people, so that you not share in her sins, and so that you not receive of her plagues." Revelation 18:4b

Our walk with Christ is an individual walk. While we may very well have the fellowship of other Believers, we might otherwise be alone. Each one of us individually will give an account of himself before our Creator.

"But why do you judge your brother? Or why do you treat your brother as being of no account? For everyone shall appear before the judgment seat of Christ." Romans 14:10

"So then each of us shall give account concerning himself to God." Romans 14:12

There are times when taking a stance for Christ can mean the loss of friends and family members.

"He who loves father or mother more than Me is not worthy of Me. And he who loves son or daughter more than Me is not worthy of Me." Matthew 10:37

"And everyone who has left houses or brothers or sisters or father or mother or wife or children or lands, for My name, shall receive a hundredfold, and inherit eternal life." Matthew 19:29

But nonetheless keep these verses in mind…

"When my father and my mother forsake me, then Jehovah will gather me up." Psalms 27:10

"Yet I have left in Israel seven thousand, all whose knees have not bowed to Baal, and every mouth that has not kissed him." 1st Kings 19:18

Amen!

Chapter 9

Christmas Tree

As with the origins of most all religiously celebrated 'Christian' holy days there are often different historical backgrounds to traditions that often were mixed with various cultures to form what is now known. Pagan nations often kept many of their pagan traditions and 'christianized' them while the Roman Catholic Church (RCC) heavily participated in continuing a good majority of such traditions while giving so-called Christian themes to them. This bible study is going to take an in-depth look at the origin of the "christmas tree".

Every year people all over the world purchase a tree, decorate it with lights and often an angel on top, and display this tree as the centerpiece of their living room. What exactly does a tree have to do with the birth of Jesus?

One origin of the tree was "an early Roman ritual...to exchange green tree branches on January 1. They believed this would bring them good luck."[1] Another was the Scandinavian's who worshipped evergreen trees. "They believed god-like spirits inhabited them so people brought trees into their homes to please the spirits and seek their blessing."[2]

The tree entered America through the German immigrants. The popular origin of the "christmas tree" stems from a German, Martin Luther (1483-1546). "One clear, brisk Christmas Eve, Martin Luther was walking home under the star-studded sky. It was so wonderful. As he walked he tried to think how he could catch the beauty of the eve and bring it home to his children. Suddenly he thought of a large evergreen tree gleaming with candles. He proceeded to find a tree, cut it down and take it home to decorate it. His children were delighted. Hence we have the beginnings of our modern 'Christmas Tree' with all the trimmings."[3] However with a little bit of research we can easily prove that Martin Luther was not the only one to ever think of putting a tree in the home with candles on it. In fact, as we will soon learn, this stems from a much older tradition. Take a look at your Christ 'mass' lights, they still resemble miniature candles.

In Jeremiah 10:3-4 we learn that the worship of trees is spoken against, long before the birth of Jesus Christ, our Lord. *"For the customs of the people are vain; for one cuts a tree out of the forest with the ax, the work of the hands of the craftsman. They make it beautiful with silver and gold they fasten it with nails and hammers, so that it will not totter."*[4]

Modern books often leave out much of the historical facts regarding the origins of Christ 'mass' and the traditions that go along with it. In order to make this bible study the author has sought various sources of information that was obtained largely through the Chicagoland area libraries where old books may still be found and cited. The following information comes from such a book.

"A Scandinavian myth of great antiquity speaks of a 'service-tree' sprung from the blood-drenched soil where two lovers had been killed by violence. At certain nights in the Christmas season mysterious lights were seen flaming in its branches that no wind could extinguish."[5]

"The French have their legend as well. In a romance of the thirteenth century the hero finds a gigantic tree whose branches are covered with burning candles, some standing erect, the others upside down, and on the top the vision of a child with a halo around his curly head. The knight asked the Pope for an explanation, who declared that the tree undoubtedly represented mankind, the child the Saviour, and the candles good and bad human beings."[6]

"Wolfram von Eschenbach, the famous minstrel, sings of a prevailing custom of welcoming guests with branches ornamented with burning candles."[7]

As stated before Martin Luther was certainly not the first to come up with the idea of having a decorated tree. "An older German legend makes St. Winfrid the inventor of the idea. In the midst of a crowd of converts he hewed down a giant oak which had formerly been the object of their Druidic worship. 'Then the sole wonder in Winfrid's life came to pass. For as the bright blade circled above his head, and the flakes of wood flew from the deepening gash in the body of the tree, a whirling wind passed over the forest. It gripped the oak from its foundations. Backward it fell like a tower, groaning as it split asunder in four pieces. But just behind it, and unharmed by the ruin, stood a young fir-tree, pointing a green spire towards the stars. Winfrid let the axe drop, and turned to speak to the people. 'This little tree, a young child of the forest, shall be your holy tree to-night. It is wood of peace, for your houses are built of the fir. It is the sign of an endless life, for it leaves are ever green. See how it points upward to heaven. Let this be called the tree of the Christ-child; gather about it, not in the wild wood, but in your own homes; there it will shelter no deeds of blood, but loving gifts and rites of kindness.'"[8]

The tree "…may have some remote connection with the great tree Yggdrasil of Norse mythology. It may be a revival of the pine-trees in the Roman Saturnalia which were decorated with images of Bacchus, as described by Virgil in the Georgics:"[9]

> *In jolly hymns they praise the god of wine,*
> *Whose earthen images adorn the pine,*
> *And these are hung on high in honor of the vine.*
> *(Dryden's translation.)*

He continues, "Two other suggestions are offered by Sir George Birdswood in the *Asiatic Quarterly Review* (vol. i. pp. 19-20) 'It has been explained', he says, 'as being derived from the ancient Egyptian practice of decking houses at the time of the winter solstice with branches of the date-palm, the symbol of life triumphant over death, and therefore of perennial life in the renewal of each bounteous year; and the supporters of these suggestions point to the fact that pyramids of green paper, covered all over with wreaths and festoons of flowers and strings of sweetmeats, are often substituted in Germany for the Christmas tree. But similar pyramids, together with similar trees, the latter usually altogether artificial, and often constructed of the costliest materials, even of gems and gold, are carried about at marriage ceremonies in India and at many festivals, such as the Huli, or annual festival of the vernal equinox. These pyramids represent Mount Meru and the earth, and the trees, the Kalpadrama, or Tree of Ages, and the fragrant Parijata, the tree of every perfect gift, which grew on the slopes of Mount Meru; and in their inlarged sense they symbolize the splendor of the outstretched heavens, as of a tree, laden with golden fruit, deep-rooted in the earth. Both pyramids and trees are also phallic emblems of life, individual, terrestrial, and celestial. Therefore, if a relationship exists between the Egyptian practice of decking houses at the winter solstice with branches of the date-palm, and the German and English customs of using gift-bearing and brilliantly illuminated evergreen trees, which are nearly always firs, as a Christmas decoration, it is most probably due to collateral rather than to direct descent; and this is indicated by the Egyptians having regarded the date-palm not only as an emblem of immortality, but also of starlit firmament.'"[10]

"The suggestion as to collateral rather than direct descent is eminently plausible. The legends already quoted show that even in medieval times there was a tradition of holiness investing an illuminated tree which made it mystically appropriate to the season of the winter solstice...about this time the Jews celebrated their feats of Chanuckah (q. v.), or Lights, also known as the Feast of the Dedication. Lighted candles are a feature of the Jewish feast. Innumerable lights must therefore have been twinkling in every Jewish house in Bethlehem and Nazareth at about the reputed time of the Saviour's birth. It is worthy of note that the German name for Christmas is Weihnacht, the Night of Dedication, and that the Greeks call Christmas the Feast of Lights. These vague traditions margining together finally led to the permanent establishment of the Christmas-tree. As a regular institution, however, it can be traced back only to the sixteenth century. During the Middle Ages it suddenly appears in Strassburg. A valuable authentic manuscript of 1608, by a Strassburg burgher, now in a private collection in Friedberg, Hesse, describes the tree as a feature of the Christmas season. The manuscript of a book entitled 'The Milk of Catechism,' by the Strassburg theologian Dannbauer, mentions the same subject in a similar way. For two hundred years the fashion maintained itself along the Rhine, when suddenly, at the beginning of this century, it spread all over Germany, and fifty years later had conquered Christendom." [11]

"The first description of a Christmas-tree in modern literature is to be found in 'The Nut-Cracker,' a fairy-tale by Fouque and Hofffmann."[12]

"In 1830 the Christmas-tree was introduced by Queen Caroline into Munich. At the same time it beat its path through Bohemia into Hungary, where it became fashionable among the Magyar aristocracy. In 1840 the Duchess Helena of Orleans, brought it to the Tuileries. Empress Eugenie also patronized it, but the middle class it was still considered an intruder of Alsatian origin. In 1860 the German residents of Paris could procure a Christmas-tree only with the greatest difficulty. However, nine years later the trees were regularly sold in the market."[13] Furthermore, "It was the marriage of Queen Victoria to a German prince which led to the introduction of the German custom into England."[14]

A more modern source concurs "Baal-Berith (the Babylonian Tammuz) was symbolized as an evergreen, or immortal tree. The Christmas tree, then decked with gold (deity), and silver (unlimited provision), represents the deified, reincarnation life of Nimrod, which has sprung forth from the dead tree stump."[15] From yet another online source the following information is cited, "Since the earliest of times, trees, especially green evergreens, were worshipped by the pagans. To them it represented life and freshness. Since it was EVER green, it always had life. The trees were worshipped as symbols as symbols of life, fertility, sexual potency and reproduction (emphasis in original)."[16]

Referring back to another old source we turn to Alexander Hislop. He has this to say about the origin of the Christ 'mass' tree, "the Christmas tree, now so common amoung us, was equally common in PAGAN ROME AND PAGAN EGYPT (emphasis in original). In Egypt that tree was the palm tree; in Rome it was the fir; the palm tree denoting the Pagan Messiah as Baal-Tamar the fir referring to him as Ball-Berith. The mother of Adonis, the sun god and great mediatorial divinity, was mystically said to have been changed into a TREE, and when in that state to have brought forth her divine son. If the mother was a tree, the son must have been recognized as the 'Man the branch.' And this entirely accounts for putting the Yule Log into the fire on Christmas-eve, and the appearance of the Christmas tree the next morning. The Christmas tree, as has been stated, was generally at Rome a different tree, even the fir; but the very same idea as was implied in the palm-tree was implied in the Christmas fir; for that covertly symbolized the new-born god as BAAL-BERITH, 'Lord of the Covenant,' and thus shadowed forth the perpetuity and everlasting nature of his power, now that after having fallen before his enemies, he has risen triumphant over them all. Therefore, the 25th of December, the day that was observed at Rome as the day when the victorious god appeared on earth, was held as the Natalis invicti solis, 'The birthday of the Unconquerable Sun. Now the Yule Log is the dead stock of Nimrod, deified as the sun god, but cut down by his enemies; the Christmas tree is Nimrod redivivus – the slain god comes to life again."[17]

Please note here that in different cultures the same pagan gods were often worshipped with different names. Once again a modern source will be cited for the final time. "The first decorating of an evergreen tree was done by pagans in honor of their god Adonis, who after being slain was brought to life by the serpent Aesculapius. The representation of this slain god was a dead stump of a tree. Around this stump coiled the snake Aesculapius symbol of life restoring. And lo – from the roots of the dead tree comes forth another and different tree – an evergreen tree symbolic to pagans of a god who cannot die! In Egypt this god was worshipped in a palm tree as Baal-Tamar. The fir tree was worshipped in Rome as the same new born god as Baal-Berith, who was restored to life by the same serpent, and a feast was held in honor of him on December 25th called the 'Birthday of the unconquered Sun.' Now in Babylon's 'Mystery' system of idol worship the sun was called 'Baal,'...so when Tammuz the son of the queen of heaven was worshiped as God he was also reverenced by the name of Baal. ....the Roman Catholic Church has brought down through the ages to us, the paganism of

Baal or the worship of the sun, mingled with the worship of Aesculapius the serpent."[18]

Once again referring back to a few more pieces of information contained in old books we will finish up with the origin of the Christ 'mass' tree. As with the lights that are put on the tree this source sheds some light, no pun intended, on the situation. "The lighting of it with candles undoubtedly grew out of the belief that candles appeared miraculously on various trees at the Christmas season."[19] Going back to not only the tree itself but a brief mention of the origins of the green (oft times another color) garland that also accompanies many homes the following information is bestowed, "the decking of churches, houses, and shops with evergreens at Christmas, springs from a period far anterior to the revelation of Christianity, and seems proximately to be derived from the customs prevalent during the Saturnalia of the inhabitants of Rome ornamenting their temples and dwelling with green boughs. From this latter circumstance, we find several early ecclesiastical councils prohibiting the members of the church to imitate the pagans in thus ornamenting their houses. But in process of time, the pagan custom was like others of a similar origin, introduced into and incorporated with the ceremonies of the church itself. The sanction of our Saviour likewise came to be pleaded for the practice, he having entered Jerusalem in triumph amid the shouts of the people, who strewed palm-branches in his way. It is evident that the use of flowers and green boughs as a means of decoration, is almost instinctive in human nature, and we accordingly find scarcely any nation, civilized or savage, with which it has not become more or less familiar. The Jews employed it in their Feast of Tabernacles, in the month of September; the ancient Druids and other Celtic nations hung up the mistletoes and green branches of different kinds over their doors to propitiate the woodland spirits; and a similar usage prevailed, as we have seen, in Rome." Continuing, "Stow, that invaluable chronicler, informs us in his Survey of London, that 'against the feast of Christmas every man's house, as also their parish churches, were decked with holme (the evergreen oak), ivy, bayes, and whatsoever the season of year afforded to be green. The conduits and standards in the streets were likewise garnished: among the which I read, that in the year 1444, by tempest of thunder and lightning, towards the morning of Candlemas-day, at the Leadenhall, in Cornhill, a standard of tree, being set up in the midst of the pavement, fast in the ground, nailed full of holme and ivie, for disport of Christmas to the people, was torne up and cast downe by the malignant spirit (as was thought), and the stones of the pavement all about were cast in the streets, and into divers houses, so that the people were sore aghast at the great tempest.'"[20]

Now that an in-depth look at the various origins of the Christ 'mass' tree have been stated the following question must be asked. Which of the origins had a Christian origin? Well the answer is none, in fact the origin of the Christ 'mass' tree predates the birth of Jesus. Please note that this study only covers one aspect of one holiday. So what do Christians do in regards to this pagan practice? From here let's explore the Holy Scriptures and see what God has to say regarding pagan practices.

"And it came to pass, as soon as Gideon was dead, that the children of Israel turned back and committed adultery with the Baals, and established Baal-Berith as their god." Judges 8:33

"But the path of the just is as the brightness of dawn, that keeps getting brighter until it is fully daytime. The way of the wicked is darkness; they do not know at what they stumble." Proverbs 4:18-19

"For we must all appear before the judgment seat of Christ, that each one may receive the things done in the body, according to what he has done whether good or bad." 2 Corinthians 5:10

"You shall not follow the majority in doing evil..." Exodus 23:2a

"You shall burn the graven images of their gods with fire; you shall not covet the silver or gold that is on them, nor take it for yourselves, lest you be snared by it; for it is an abomination to Jehovah your God. Nor shall you bring an abomination into your house, lest you be utterly destroyed like it. You shall detest it unto

abomination and loathe it unto abhorrence, for it is a prohibited thing." Deuteronomy 7:25-26

"take heed to yourself that you are not ensnared to follow them, after they are destroyed before you, and that you do not inquire after their gods, saying, How did these nations serve their gods? I also will do likewise. You shall not do so unto Jehovah your God; for everything that is an abomination to Jehovah which He has hated, they have done unto their gods; for they burn even their sons and daughters in the fire unto their gods." Deuteronomy 12:30-31

"To whom then will you compare the Mighty God? Or what likeness will you compare to Him?" Isaiah 40:18

"Whoever is too poor for such an offering chooses a tree that will not rot; he looks for a skillful workman to prepare a graven image that will not totter.: Isaiah 40:20

"To whom then will you compare Me, or with who am I equal? Says the Holy One." Isaiah 40:25

A reminder that nowhere in the Word of God are we told to remember the birth of our Lord Jesus Christ. We are commanded to remember His death, however. (*Luke 22:18-19; 1 Corinthians 11:23-26*)

This bible study will close with the following verses.

"And what agreement has Christ with Belial?" 2 *Corinthians 6:15a*

"But test all things; hold fast what is good. Abstain from every form of evil." 2 Thessalonians 5:21-22

"Come out of her, my people, so that you not share in her sins, and so you not receive of her plagues." Revelation 18:4b

A final thought:

"For preventing disorders, arising in several places within this jurisdiction by reason of some still observing such festivals as were superstitiously kept in other communities, to the great dishonor of God and offense of others: it is therefore ordered by this court and the authority thereof that whosoever shall be found observing any such day as Christmas or the like, either by forbearing of labor, feasting, or any other way, upon any such account as aforesaid, every such person so offending shall pay for every such offence five shilling as a fine to the county."

From the records of the General Court,
Massachusetts Bay Colony
May 11, 1659

Bibliography

Chapter 1
1. The Book of Days, Chambers, 1879
2. Ibid.
3. Ibid.
4. Ibid.
5. Ibid.
6. Ibid.
7. Ibid.
8. Ibid
9. Unknown Source
10. Ibid.
11. Ibid.
12. Ibid.
13. Curiosities of Popular Customs, Walsh, 1897
14. Ibid.
15. Ibid.
16. Ibid.

Chapter 2
1. Book of Days, Chambers, 1879
2. Ibid.
3. Ibid.
4. Ibid.
5. Ibid.

Chapter 3
1. The Book of Days, Chambers, 1879
2. Ibid.
3. Ibid.
4. Ibid.
5. Ibid.
6. Ibid.
7. Ibid.
8. Unknown

Chapter 4
1. http://www.logosresourcepages.org/good_friday.htm
2. Ibid.
3. Ibid.
4. Ibid.
5. Ibid.
6. Ibid.
7. Ibid.
8. Ibid.
9. Ibid.

Chapter 5
1. Book of Days, Chambers, 1879
2. Ibid.
3. Ibid.
4. Ibid.
5. Ibid.
6. Ibid.
7. Ibid.
8. Ibid.

Chapter 6
1. Webster's University Dictionary Unabridged, 1942, The World Publishing Company
2. Curiosities of Popular Customs, 1925, Walsh
3. ??? The American Book of Days, 1948, Williams
4. Dictionary of Christian Antiquities, 1875, Smith & Cheetham
5. Pagan Traditions, 2000, Ingraham
6. http://www.gilead.net/bible/christmas8.htm
7. Ibid.
8. http://users.aol.com/libcfl/easter.htm
9. Curiosities of Popular Customs, 1925, Walsh
10. ??? The American Book of Days, 1948, Williams
11. Pagan Traditions, 2000, Ingraham
12. Ibid.
13. All About American Holidays, p.103, Krythe
14. Pagan Traditions, 2000, Ingraham
15. Lilies, Rabbits and Painted Eggs, p.51, Barth
16. ??? The American Book of Days, 1948, Williams

17. Ibid.

18. Ibid.

19. Curiosities of Popular Customs, 1925, Walsh

20. http://www.gilead.net/bible/christmas8.htm

21. ??? The American Book of Days, 1948, Williams

22. Lilies, Rabbits and Painted Eggs, p.51, Barth

23. Rabbits, Eggs, and Other Easter Errors, pp.11-12, Tardo

24. Celebrations, p.105, Myers

25. http://www.a-voice.org/qa/pagan.htm#sunrise

Chapter 7

1. Curiosities of Popular Customs, Walsh, 1898

2. Ibid.

3. Ibid.

4. Ibid.

5. Ibid.

6. Ibid.

7. Ibid.

8. Ibid.

9. Ibid.

10. Ibid.

11. Ibid.

12. thefreedictionary.com

13. Curiosities of Popular Customs, Walsh, 1898

14. Ibid.

15. http:www.lasttrumpetministries.org/tracts/tract6.html, Last Trumpet Ministries, Pastor David Meyer, Beaver Dam, WI

Chapter 8

1. http://en.wikipedia.org/wiki/Bethlehem#Climate

2. Adam Clarke's Commentary on the Bible (Luke 2:8)

3. Alexander Hislop, The Two Babylons or The Papal Worship, Loizeaux Brothers, 1916, pp. 94, 97.

4. Ibid. pp.93

5. Logos Communication Consortium, Christmas – What makes it important?, Brochure

6. http://en.wikipedia.org/wiki/Winter_solstice

7. Curiosities of Popular Customs, Walsh, 1897

8. Ibid.

9. Ibid.
10. Ibid.
11. Ibid.
12. Ibid.
13. Ibid.
14. The Book of Days, Chambers, 1879
15. Ibid.
16. Ibid.
17. Ibid.
18. Ibid.
19. Ibid.
20. Ibid.
21. Ibid.
22. Unknown
23. Unknown
24. Unknown 2
25. Unknown 2
26. Unknown 2
27. Unknown 2
28. MacMillan Compact Encyclopedia
29. www.gilead.net*
30. Ibid.
*Please note this website is part of the SDA church and I do not
recommend it.

*Note: British English is left as is, therefore in some words a 'u' is
had where it would not be in the American English language.*

Chapter 9

1. Logos Communication Consortium brochure
2. Ibid.
3. Ibid.
4. Holy Scriptures, VW, 2006
5. Curiosities of Popular Customs, Walsh, 1897
6. Ibid.
7. Ibid.
8. Ibid.
9. Ibid.
10. Ibid.

11. Ibid.
12. Ibid.
13. Ibid.
14. Ibid.
15. http://www.demonbuster.com/christmas.html
16. http://www.jesus-is-lord.com/tree.htm
17. The Two Babylons, Hislop, 1919
18. http://www.jesus-is-lord.com/christm3.htm
19. Source Unknown – Unfortunately the copies made from the original book do not include the title of the book or the author.
20. The Book of Days, Chambers, 1879

All scripture is taken from the VW 2006 edition of the Holy Scriptures.
www.a-voice.org

Made in the USA
Columbia, SC
19 November 2021

49344531R00041